D1740510

How to cast
yourself as the
STAR
in your life

By
Thom McFadden

BE THE STAR IN YOUR LIFE

LIFESTΛND

THOM McFADDEN

ACTING FOR REAL™

Excerpts from Chapter 25: *Communication* reprinted by permission of Dr. Richard Bandler, co-founder of NLP™

Selections from Chapters 24 & 26: *Survival to Success* and *Self-Perseverance* reprinted and adapted from <u>Get Rich in Spite of Yourself</u> by Louis M. Grafe, Los Angeles, Grafe & Grafe, 1945©

Copyright © 2006 by Thom McFadden

www.ActingforReal.com

All rights reserved. No part of this book may be reproduced (except for inclusion in reviews), disseminated, transmitted, or utilized in any form or by any means, electronic or mechanical, including photocopying, recording or by any information storage and retrieval system, or the Internet/ World Wide Web without permission in writing from the author or publisher.

Published by LifeStand, Inc.
Las Vegas, Nevada, United States of America
www.Lifestand.com

Printed in Canada

Design & Editorial Director, and photo captions by Gretchen Martin, Little Pearls Studio, Los Angeles, CA

*Book Design by   Arbor Books, Inc.
19 Spear Road, Suite 202
Ramsey, NJ 07446
www.arborbooks.com*

Cover Design by DeatsDesign.com, Woodland Hills, CA

Library of Congress Control Number: 2006906913
ISBN: 0-9788214-0-8
   1.   Title 2. Author 3. Self-Help/ Motivational/ Success

To my Wife, my Life…
Nancy

Nancy McFadden

Photographed at a celebration for the American
Children's Theater co-founded by Thom and Nancy
McFadden

Portrait of Thom by actor and artist Fred Ward

CONTENTS

ACT TWO
THE CREATIVE WHEEL OF EXCELLENCE

ACT THREE
THE ACTOR FOR REAL'S TOOLBOX

To the Actor for Real:

Heaven Hi! I congratulate you on taking these positive steps toward attaining fulfillment in your life. For over 30 years, I have used the techniques and strategies in this book to teach actors how to create characters for the stage and screen. Now I am excited to share the same techniques with you, the Actor for Real. Over the years as an actor, teacher, and coach, it has become very apparent to me that acting is turning the psychology of a character into behavior. Why then, can't a layperson, by modeling external behavior and connecting it to his internal psychology, learn how to portray empowering characters in life by using the same strategies and techniques that an actor uses for the stage and screen? Now you can! I hope that this book will stimulate your imagination and challenge you to take action.

Be Bop!
Thom McFadden

ACKNOWLEDGMENTS

No one writes a book alone. Most of the ideas in this book are mine while a few are from other sources long forgotten. I wish to acknowledge the immeasurable contribution others have made to my life by freely sharing their enlightenment. It is my sincere desire that you may benefit from the ideas contained in this book and pass them on to others.

Thank you Gretchen Martin for helping me to complete this book, and Tyler McFadden, James McFadden and Christine Whitmarsh for your invaluable contributions. I am grateful for the love and loyalty so generously given to me by Brian Hamill, J.C. (Justine) Compton, Tim Matheson, Fred Ward, Jay Dekeyser, Genevieve Bujold, Alex Street, Jim Beckett, George DiCenzo, Francesca and Rudy Bianci, Andrea Tose, Tracy Tracton, Jan Cady, Candy and Michael Wahl, Rita and Larry Miller, David Tod, Fran Tarkenton, and Paul Donner. Throughout our years of friendship, I have been uplifted by your support, nourished by your love, and inspired by your examples.

I wish to acknowledge Dr.Richard Bandler, co-founder of NLP™, who has graciously given me permission to use his work in sub-modalities as part of my teachings in this book. Richard has been a great influence to me creatively, and has left an indelible mark on my life.

I wish to thank my late mother for the love, encouragement, and respect that she has so generously given me. My Aunt Vesta for taking me in and loving me like one of her own. Judy McFadden, who has been more like a sister than a cousin. Fred and Nancy Tod, for their love and support.

And finally, I'd like to thank my family, my three sons James, Tyler, and Will, who contribute to my personal growth and happiness every day, and my wonderful wife Nancy for being the leading lady in my life.

There are so many others who have made a difference, whom I wish to thank. You know who you are. However, I feel like I'm at the Academy Awards and the music is playing me off, so…Let's Act!

For years I've been teaching actors
to be real people.
Now I'm teaching real people
to be actors.

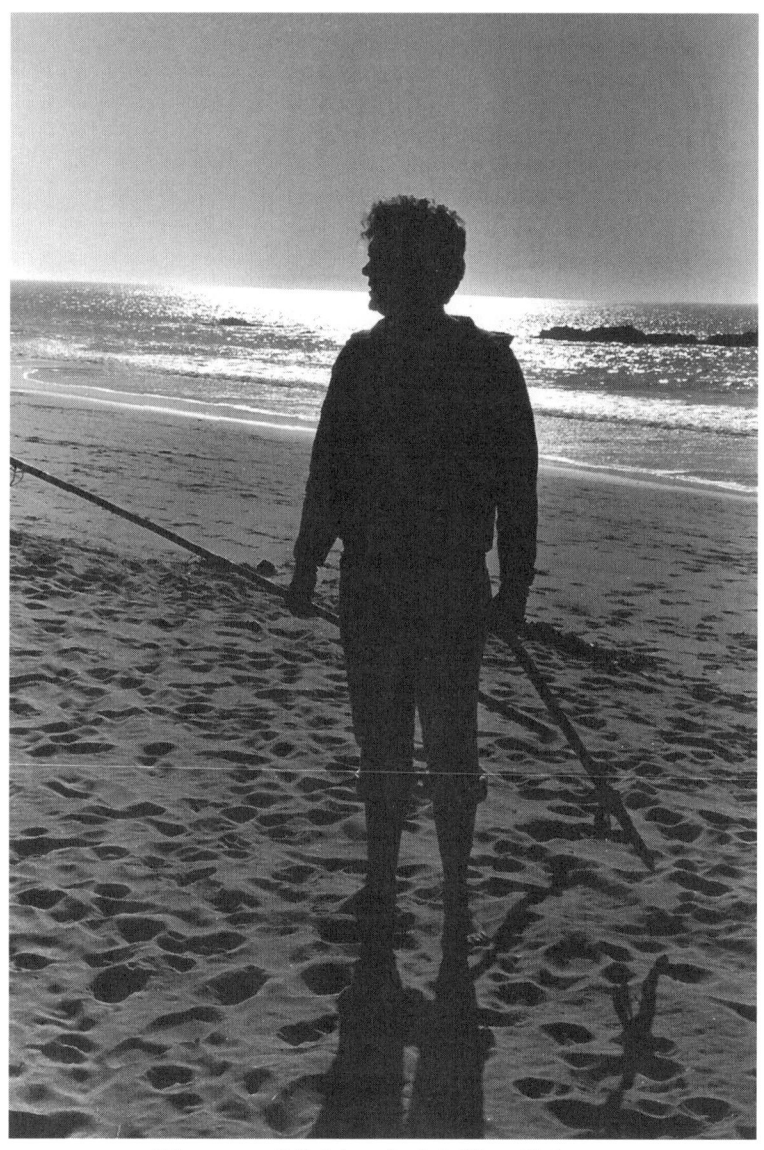

Thom surf fishing in Malibu Colony

Photo by Brian Hamill

"All the world's a stage,
And all the men and women merely players;
They have their exits and their entrances,
And one man in his time plays many parts..."
                                                                                    —William Shakespeare

INTRODUCTION

When I first arrived in Los Angeles, I was fortunate enough to rent a beach house in Malibu. Living so near the ocean, I was able to enjoy my passion for surf fishing. My neighbor Archibald Leach would often join me as I fished, and we would sit talking about life, acting, and the catch of the day.

Archibald emphasized to me the importance of constantly working on yourself as an actor: "An actor needs to mine the gold in himself," he would say, "Life is a stage, and we all role-play various personalities in our everyday lives. Every one of us should prospect their own unique talents." He spoke in depth about working in the circus as an acrobat, juggler, and barker to develop the skills he would need to be a successful entertainer.

Archibald was a great example of how far you can go by creating a character that empowers you. He spent many years portraying the "professional actor" character in his artistic life. Archibald's wisdom taught me to tap into the "gold" by building on my strengths and instincts as an actor. I will never forget fishing with Archibald Leach as he told me how he had spent a lifetime creating his character in life, "Cary Grant."

THE ACTOR FOR REAL

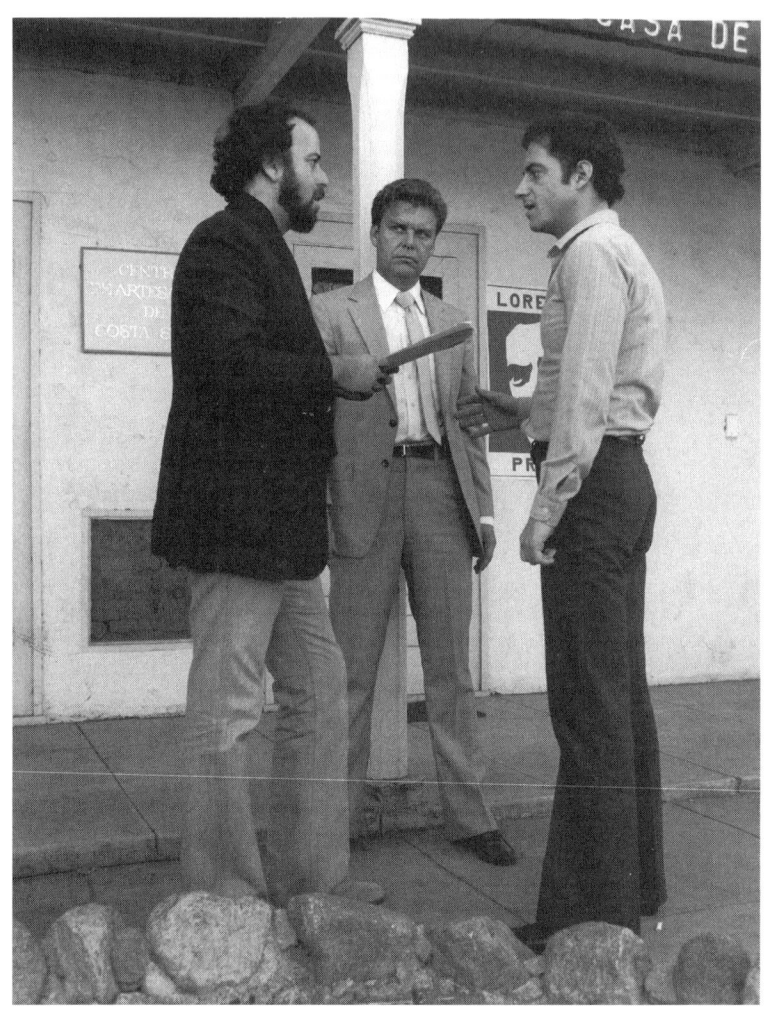

BE COACHABLE

Ray Sharky and Thom working with Academy
Award nominee, writer and director James Toback
on the 1982 feature film *Love and Money*

CHAPTER 1
BE COACHABLE

"We know what we are, but know not what we may be."
        —Shakespeare

"The ideal condition
Would be, I admit, that men should be right by instinct;
But since we are all likely to go astray,
The reasonable thing is to learn from those who can teach."
        —Sophocles

My success as an actor, teacher, author, coach and parent has been due in a large part to my willingness to learn from great mentors. I have been fortunate enough to model and grow from the knowledge, experience, and wisdom of Henry Miller, J.C. (Justine) Compton, William Inge, Jack Garfein, Rod Steiger, Paul Donner, Dr. Richard Bandler and Cary Grant. I could not have achieved my professional and personal success without their help. From them, I learned to be ecstatic and possessed about my outcomes everyday.

A coach can help you create a positive attitude, bust out of comfort zones, change limiting beliefs, and teach you how to model excellence. He helps you to make changes and encourages you to build strength where strength lies, while constantly inspiring you towards your desired goals. He gives you the necessary third eye to see things in your career, your life, and your craft from a greater perspective.

Through your willingness and my coaching, we will identify the characters that you portray in life (or lack thereof), utilizing the same strategies and techniques that an actor uses to develop characters for the stage or screen. This process teaches you how to create new, empowering characters to STAR in your life, thereby maximizing your potential for success.

Do you have a need to better yourself? Of course you do, or you wouldn't be reading this book. Are you coachable? Let's find out!

The phenomenal Tiger Woods' incredible achievements as a golfer are a perfect example of natural talent taken to new levels of greatness through coaching. Tiger not only consistently wins high stakes tournaments, but also frequently sets records and has become the youngest champion ever to win The Masters. He has already established himself as one of the greatest golfers in sports history.

Tiger Woods, even with all of his skill and talent, still has a coach—in fact, he has many coaches, on and off the links. Tiger's most important coach was his late father, Earl Woods, a military man who taught him to dedicate himself to the discipline that an athlete must have to win. Tiger Woods is just one example of a willing student being taught by great coaches. Anyone who has reached the pinnacle of success would not have been able to do so without great coaching.

The aim of this book is to lend you the power of an experienced (and hopefully somewhat entertaining) coach to make your outcomes positive, progressive, accelerated and aligned with your goals!

An important thing to remember is that there are no such things as failures, there are only outcomes. Your beliefs, attitudes, and actions are directly responsible for your outcomes.

When I coach actors for a role, I have them first read the play or screenplay for logic, then write down their first impressions. As an Actor for Real, it's important for you to do the same. Get a pen and pad of paper ready and start your Acting for Real journal of your first impressions and observations to keep beside you as you continue to read.

Before moving on to the next chapter, jot down your first impressions of all that you've read to this point and what's applicable to making changes *now*. Make sure that you do this after each chapter because there may be a pop quiz at the end! Ha-ha.

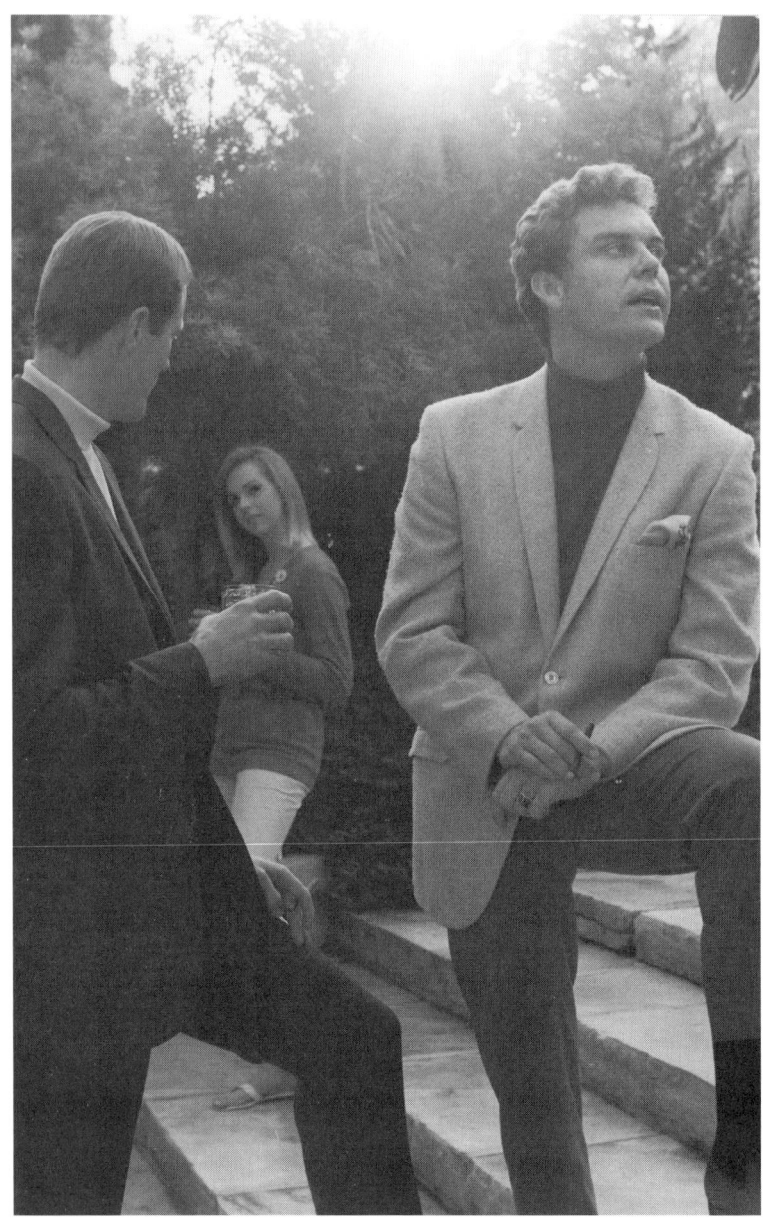

ATTITUDE

Thom's modeling days…
It's all about the attitude!

CHAPTER 2
THE ACTING FOR REAL ATTITUDE

"If you don't change your beliefs, your life will be like this forever."
                                                    —Unknown

When an actor like Tom Cruise, Denzel Washington, Meryl Streep, Gwyneth Paltrow, Brad Pitt, Reese Witherspoon, or Russel Crowe, works on a part, they completely immerse themselves in the life of the character that has been written by the screenwriter. They create a backstory, using the character's values, ambitions, habits, ticks, strengths, weaknesses, likes and dislikes; everything that has to do with the character's behavior in the given circumstances. This process is called downtime. Downtime is when the actor researches what the character is made of, turning the psychology of the character into behavior. Uptime, or real time, begins when the director calls, "Action!" so that the behavior of the character becomes organic. We will explore this further in the second act of this book.

Since you are the star in your life, your downtime is understanding the backstory and psychology of the characters that you portray. The first step in nuking the negative characters and replacing them with new empowered ones is developing the Acting for Real attitude.

ACTING FOR REAL

at·ti·tude (n.)
1. A manner of acting, feeling, or thinking that shows one's disposition, opinion, etc.
2. A position of the body or manner of carrying oneself.

The more I study, write, teach, coach, and direct, the more I'm convinced that a great attitude, positive belief system, and self-confidence will allow you to consistently reach your goals. To tap into your creative mind, you must first understand how to grasp a positive attitude with certainty. A positive attitude results from the elimination of negative thinking.

It all begins with attitude. Your attitude has a profound impact on the quality of your life. It can make or break you. Your reactions to events that happen in your life are far more important than the actual events. You cannot change the past or predict the future. Challenges will continue to occur in your life. The only thing you have complete control over each and every day is your attitude. Your attitude about yourself is the perfect place to start. Each of us is born with unlimited potential. Your self-esteem is a function of the continuum between your beliefs, values, and your actions. Act with integrity.

You don't have to be the smartest or the most talented, but you do have to have a great attitude if you desire to be successful.

A great **Attitude** + a little bit of **Aptitude** =
Altitude (A + A = A)

You can go as high as you desire!

As you examine your behavior, roles, and hidden agreements, you will learn more about yourself and you will disengage from self-limiting (negative) attitudes. Once you have eliminated those obstacles, you will be on the road to the positive attitude and enlightened state of mind that will serve as your foundation as an Actor for Real.

Acting, like life, is about making choices and stringing them together. You make choices everyday that affect your outcomes. Every morning you have the opportunity to have a great attitude or a lousy one. If you wake up on the wrong side of the bed, roll over, and start your day off right. The choice is yours!

Be Possessed

pos·sessed (adj.)
  1. Controlled by, or as if by, a spirit or other force.
  2. Influenced or controlled by a powerful force such as a strong emotion; obsessed.

In my acting seminars, I begin by asking, "Who wants to be a movie star?" Every hand goes up. "If it took only one word to make it happen—would you do it?" Everyone shouts, "Yes! Tell us the word!"

I usually make students wait until the end of the seminar to find out, but I'll give it to you right now…the mystery word that will accomplish anything you desire is (drum roll please) POSSESSED. To be *possessed* is not to *want* to be a movie star, but to *need* to be a movie star!

ACTING FOR REAL

Show me any successful person and I will show you a person that is possessed.

Their success is driven by great desire, a positive attitude, and an intense love of their work.

In order to make successful changes in your behavior, you must put yourself in a state of mind—present, positive, and *possessed*– that is so powerful, that the changes you are making no longer seem like an effort.

You cannot drive yourself to success. You must be driven to be possessed!

You must be possessed about the goals you have set for yourself, in order to reach them via the steps presented in this book.

The process involves becoming aware of, and learning to control the self-limiting, negative attitudes that stand in the way of success: Fear, Your Inner Critic, and Self-Talk. Let's start by understanding fear.

Fear

fear (n.)
1. A feeling of agitation and anxiety caused by the presence or imminence of danger;
2. A state or condition marked by this feeling
3. A feeling of disquiet or apprehension.

"It is what we fear that happens to us."
                                            —Oscar Wilde

"Fear is excitement without breath."
—Robert Heller

Once you are possessed, identifying and conquering fear is the next step towards attaining a positive attitude. Fear can be a self-limiting emotion when it is used as an excuse to stop moving forward. Imagine two boys, with similar athletic ability, playing football. When an opposing player kicks the ball, the first boy thinks to himself, *"I hope he kicks it to me! My family is watching, I feel alert, and I know I can run for the touchdown!"* While the second boy is thinking, *"I hope he doesn't kick it to me. I'm not ready yet and my dad's watching...if I fumble he's going to kill me! Please God, don't let him kick it to me!"*

One boy has faith in his abilities, and he turns his fear into anticipation that he will catch the ball and run it back for a touchdown. The second boy is frightened of his abilities and is frozen by fear, hoping that the ball won't be kicked to him because he's afraid he'll drop it.

This is not to say that the boy who runs for the ball is not afraid. The major difference is that the first boy uses his fear and adrenaline as momentum, to propel him down the field. He's confident that he's going to score a touchdown. The other boy allows the fear to freeze him in his tracks, eliminating any chance of success.

Fear is an emotion that, when combined with a positive belief system and a healthy attitude, will drive you forward throughout your life. As an Actor for Real, fear is a healthy, natural reaction that helps you anticipate what is coming next, confront it, handle it, and continue on toward your goals. Fear places you in present time, reminding you that you are in the now.

A stage actor waiting for his entrance from the wings must place himself in the upcoming scene, run through its events in his head, and prepare himself emotionally before taking the stage. The actor backstage is full of anticipation, charged with adrenaline, and yes, he is afraid. That fear will drive him throughout the scene, making him alert, and ready for whatever happens next on that stage. Without it he will be unready, unprepared, and unable to react to the events that unfold. Fear is one of the emotions that will direct him to a positive outcome. If you replace the word "fear" with "anticipation" it will transform into a positive driving force that stimulates your imagination and propels you toward success.

Simply trying to "fight" natural human responses such as fear is rarely effective. Instead, you must befriend your fear and use it as a tool to empower you.

Thom as a toddler. You can see Thom's anticipation
as older brother, O'Brian, tries to hold him back!

ACTING FOR REAL

Inner Critic

Like fear, self-limiting beliefs are also created by your inner critic. This internal voice talks you out of going after things that you know you can do, you desire, and you deserve. It is inspired by the voice of someone who has told you that you can't do something —a family member, a friend, a colleague, etc. These are people who believe they are looking out for your best interests and are keeping you from getting hurt. But people like this, who are overly critical and believe they are helping you, are not aware of the psychological damage that is being done. *"You can't sing!" "Why can't you be more like your sister, she always gets good grades." "You'll never make it." "That kind of thing should be left to the professionals."* These are examples of external garbage that creates your inner critic, making it into the voice of opposition that prevents you from taking action. Once created, you feed it simply by agreeing with it, allowing it to stop you from moving forward.

Your inner critic exists because your subconscious believes it to be your protector, for better or worse. Throughout your life you have programmed your inner critic through your beliefs, environment, upbringing, and social circumstances, to resist significant changes. Therefore, when confronted with any kind of change, it believes it is protecting your best interests and keeping you from getting hurt—kind of like mom. It truly thinks that it is right.

When you start to make changes in your life and your critic questions your actions, what should you do? Most people think they have only two choices when this happens: fight it, or let it prevent you from moving forward.

When you are alone, in communion with yourself, working to make dramatic changes in your life and your critic begins to stop you, ask it to cut you some slack. Instead of fighting it and defending yourself against it, befriend your inner critic to get rid of any obstacles in your path to action. Tell it that you know it is looking out for you and trying to protect you against pain. Ask it to please let you move forward this time. This is a change that needs to be made and an action that needs to be taken to reach a positive, worthwhile outcome. Negotiate with the inner voice that is trying to keep you from taking the risk to go after what you desire in life. Ask it for some cooperation.

For instance, an actor will find lures to trick his inner critic and stimulate his creative imagination when he's playing a character. His creative imagination will allow him to portray the behavior of the character instead of shutting him down. He then turns the changes he's making into a fun game that results in the positive outcome of a multidimensional character. You can do the same!

Most people, unfortunately, follow their first instinct, which is to try to simply kill the voice. It takes far too much time to fight your inner critic, who is well armed with a lifetime of reasons *not* to change. Trying to silence your inner critic only shuts you down and paralyzes you. You are trying to ignore something that is much bigger than you—your subconscious. And when you do, you will be unable to move forward towards your goals. It's like walking in cement—the longer you pause, the harder it is to get moving again. In a state of paralysis, your critic will easily overpower you and all of the positive steps you have taken will become undone. Keep moving! Every step forward is a step in the right direction to reach your desired outcomes.

Like fear, the inner critic is a powerful force that when harnessed with a positive attitude, can inspire you to get up, dust yourself off, and keep moving forward.

Some ways to get to know and befriend your inner critic include:

- Write out all the things that your inner critic says to you at different times of the day, in different situations, and with different people, and notice what the patterns are. For example, does your inner critic get stronger when you're tired, hungry, or stressed? If so, taking breaks, unwinding, having snacks, and relaxing can all reduce the power of your inner critic.

- If writing out the inner critic's messages leads to your adding more and more criticisms to your list, stop writing and try to step back from the inner critic. See if you can simply observe that there is a part of you that thinks this way, and that not all of you thinks this way. You don't need to argue with the inner critic, just be aware of it and let it know that everything will be okay.

- Draw your inner critic like you're sketching a suspect at a crime scene. Could you pick him or her out of a lineup? If your inner critic has already spoken up and said, "You can't draw!" then capture him, don't let him get away and start drawing. What or who does the inner critic look like?

- Drawing the inner critic externalizes it and helps you to identify it when it surfaces.

- You don't have to know when your inner critic started. Just like when there's a fire you don't have to know how it started, you just have to put it out. By identifying your inner critic and befriending it, you're disarming it so that it no longer prevents you from taking action and reaching your desired outcomes.

While your inner critic acts as the preprogrammed recording of pessimism, self-talk is the internal dialogue that results.

Self-Talk

"The more man meditates upon good thoughts, the better will be his world and the world at large."
                                        —Confucius

"Every thought you've ever had is stored in your brain and remembered forever!"
                                        —Wilder Penfield

Along with your inner critic, self-talk is a constant conversation in your conscious and unconscious mind that can be self-limiting unless you become aware of it and use it to empower you. Negative self-talk can come from inside of you (inner critic) or from the outside world and the given circumstances. We are the results of how we have been programmed. The mind does not make value judgments about the information with which it is programmed. When garbage has been programmed into the subconscious, the garbage will come out—or the outcome will be garbage!

Be aware of who and what is programming your brain. Your co-stars in your life must support your beliefs and encourage your ideas so that they can help you reach your positive outcomes. If you allow bad actors to be your directors and make decisions for you, you'll be an extra rather than the star!

GARBAGE IN = GARBAGE OUT

G.I. (Misinformation)	G.O. (Limited Behavior)
1. Actors are phony	You feel uncomfortable about acting
2. Big men don't cry	Men develop stress-related illness
3. The Jones's are clumsy	Bill Jones is clumsy
4. To be an actor you've got to have IT	Lots of people miss out because they think they don't have IT

These are just a few examples of garbage in and garbage out... You get the point! Recognize your own GI = GO, so that you can stop it.

Negative Self-Talk

Negative self-talk is internal dialogue that cripples your self-esteem and promotes the victim character.

"How could I be so dumb?"
"What's wrong with me?"
"I'll never be able to act like a professional."
"I won't get far without a college degree."
"Why me? Woe is me, poor me…"

If you accept negative self-talk statements like these, you will lose your passion to succeed, excel, compete, and give back to society. By becoming aware of your self-talk, you will rekindle your passion for life and leave your victim character off stage. Through self-talk, what we are constantly thinking about and affirming to ourselves, we build and modify in our self-image. By programming our subconscious mind with positive self-talk, we can modify our current self-image, which then enables us to reach more of our true potential.

Now let's take a look at the specific roles that make up your identity.

Self-Image

"Self-image is the key to human personality and human behavior. Change the self-image and you change the personality and the behavior."
                                                                    —*Maxwell Maltz*

ACTING FOR REAL

Your self-image is based on an identity that is composed of the specific roles you play in life. The more specific characters that you identify yourself as, the more power you are feeding into your identity. When I'm doing an acting seminar, I always ask the participants, "Are you a man, woman, or a human being? You can only pick one." Most of the time they reply, "human being." WRONG! Yes we are born as humans and are beings until the day we die. But when you simply refer to yourself as a "human being," you're saying that you're a mammal who walks on two legs and currently has a heartbeat or the highest form of animal intelligence. But you are more than that, so be more than that. You are a man or a woman. You are a mother, father, brother, sister, aunt, uncle, a teacher, a pupil. You are special and unique. You portray many diverse and wonderful roles in life, so take ownership of everything that you are.

In other words, take total responsibility of your self-image as a man or a woman. Having a clear, specific sense of your identity is one of the keys to creating the positive self-image that will drive your characters to success.

Comfort Zones

Our self-image corresponds directly to behavior regulators called *comfort zones*.

For each current picture we have of ourselves there is a comfort zone that reinforces that image. There are different kinds of comfort zones. Some comfort zones come from shared images. Our culture often tells us what we should do or believe. As these images become stronger, they can become *cultural comfort zones*, or *cultural trances*. Often the strongest and most limiting comfort zones are based on personal or family values and beliefs. These are *restrictive zones*. These compelling mental maps are enough to hold people back from ever reaching out for what they need in life.

A fear of being "out of place" physically or psychologically causes us to get back into the range in which we feel most comfortable. For each current self-image picture we have, there is a corresponding comfort zone. The comfort zones regulate our behavior by allowing us to move only slightly above or below our self-image. If we move beyond these limits, we experience tension, stress, and anxiety. This tension, stress, and anxiety may only be temporary, but it is enough to discourage many people from leaving their comfort zones. Sadly, what they are missing is the emergence of a new, improved self. Comfort zones and self-image make us automatically act as we see ourselves to be.

Cultural comfort zones, or cultural trances, are when a large group of people, or entire nations, believe something and do not act in accordance with the truth. This sort of cultural comfort zone was evident in a time when the population believed the world was flat. To think otherwise was blasphemy. We still have "flat world beliefs" today: "A woman can never be president", "The world can not function without oil." These are false assumptions we make about ourselves, about others, our families or our work.

ACTING FOR REAL

Restrictive zones are the most dangerous and limiting type of comfort zone. Restrictive zones are based on strong personal rules and beliefs or family rules and beliefs. For example, "You will never be successful unless you go to college." There have been many successful people who did not go to college. Others, with this limiting restrictive zone and who never made it to college, resign themselves to failure. Restrictive zones are the most fiercely held mental maps we have. They can even be life threatening, like the restrictive zones of many who had fatal reactions to the stock market crash of 1929.

To stretch beyond your comfort zones, identify what misinformation has been programmed into you. You are not holding yourself back—your self-image is holding you back! By motivating ourselves to change and grow, we are moving away from our currently dominating self-image towards a self-image of "I can." Dissatisfaction with one's current self-image is what motivates us. We can choose the things we are dissatisfied with and the things we need to change. Our self-image is the controlling factor in how we behave because we act as we see ourselves.

Self-Esteem

"If you put a small value on yourself, rest assured that the world will not raise your price."
                                        —Unknown

The other key is how you feel about that identity: self-esteem. Whereas self-image is defined by a certainty of your identity, self-esteem is how you feel about yourself, based on your individual sense of personal worth and importance. Self-esteem is rooted in an unconditional acceptance of oneself.

Since self-esteem is a feeling, rather than an intellectual inventory of assets, changing it entails a revision of the factors of our awareness that caused this feeling of inadequacy and inferiority. A requirement for such productive self-exploration is to program yourself to maintain an awareness of your behavior, thoughts, speech, needs, actions, emotional reactions, moods, and attitudes. Only then can you make meaningful progress in expanding your awareness. During this process of self-exploration, if you're honest with yourself and refuse to believe any self-condemnation, you will soon identify the negative beliefs and observe the behaviors that are the source of low self-esteem. This will ensure that the characters you create will be built on a foundation of high self-esteem.

When an actor reveals a character at the beginning of a movie with low self-esteem, we pull for that character to make changes so that they emerge as a winner with high self-esteem in the end. One of the reasons we, the audience, root for that character as strongly as we do, is because we identify with the low self-esteem character, live vicariously through that character, and celebrate their positive outcome in the end.

ACTING FOR REAL

This book represents an opportunity for you to start to connect with your low self-esteem and distorted self-image so that you can transform your victim behavior into winning behavior, just like in the movies.

How We Feed Low Self-Esteem

The following are significant factors of awareness that not only cause low self-esteem, but also more importantly, ensure a crippling sense of inadequacy, anxiety and frustration. Recognition and understanding however, make it possible to eliminate or revise these undesirable traits. We feed low self-esteem by:

Lacking faith in our environment, our society, and ourselves.

Lacking a sense of purpose in life and thus, clear-cut goals and objectives to guide our actions.

Living in the problem, and allowing the problem to become the solution.

Depending on others for our sense of self-worth.

Failing to accept complete responsibility for our life and outcomes by not taking chances in life and not asking questions and looking for the answers.

Habitually feeding an addictive personality through self-indulgence and lack of awareness.

Playing the victim and failing to recognize that you deserve to be successful.

Requiring the "permission" of others before taking action.

Listening to our inner critic and allowing it to shut us down, indulging ourselves in self-blame, shame, guilt, and remorse.

Not allowing ourselves to look at life with a sense of humor or getting in touch with our "funny zone."

Being overly critical of others. It eventually comes back to you.

Not buying a ticket to life.

Building Self-Esteem

Most of our society passively walks around just breathing, and living in the world of, "I can't." Eliminating "I can't" and replacing it with "I can" is the action that will propel you forward to start making changes. Do this and you will handle over 50% of your low self-esteem by acknowledging that you can take action now. Low self-esteem is the weakest, most destructive foundation that any character can be built on. By taking action to create new, positive characters you are breaking the cycle of low self-esteem and are destroying your victim character.

When coaching, I encourage actors to take inventory of their personal store as a way of stocking their self-esteem. Becoming aware of your assets is a powerful method of self-exploration and a great way of building high self-esteem. As the saying goes, "If you've got it, flaunt it!" Now, what does your store have to offer?

ACTING FOR REAL

What do you need more inventory of? What needs to be reordered? The way to create product for your store, is to have a great attitude, a positive self-image, and high self-esteem. The person with high self-esteem is constantly nurturing his assets, the goods in his store, growing as an individual, and finding ways to give back to humanity. High self-esteem results from one's accepting complete responsibility for one's actions.

Self-esteem is literally a matter of life and death. It is absolutely essential for personal happiness and a rich enjoyment of life to feel good about ourselves. Here's a simple, fun acting exercise to stimulate your creative imagination and fuel your self-esteem and confidence:

MAKE YOUR MOVIE EXERCISE

Sit in a chair, close your eyes and visualize an obstacle in your life that you need to overcome (i.e., stop smoking, overeating, etc.). See yourself there—taste it, smell it, feel it, hear it! See it like a movie and you are the hero. Play out all the options. As the hero, you're able to come up with a solution to the problems you're having. If you're still stuck, go to the movie again and allow your creative imagination to move the timeline further into the future to a point where you no longer have the problem and your hero has come up with the solution. Have fun with your movie, and let your creative imagination give you the clues to overcome your obstacles and increase your self-esteem.

Have faith in yourself. Be courageous and persistent in your efforts to increase your self-esteem, and don't overanalyze ideas—analysis causes paralysis and shuts down your creative imagination!

Now that you are allowing your creative imagination to boost your self-esteem, let's keep the positive cycle going!

Self-Confidence

"As man thinketh in his heart, so is he."
—Proverbs 23:7

You are what you think.
"I am success."

Seeing yourself in a positive light (self-image) and accepting your self-worth (self-esteem) builds self-confidence. Self-confidence is confidence in one's judgment and ability.

If you have confidence in yourself, you will have the courage to venture. Having ventured, you will succeed. Having succeeded, you will gain more confidence. Having more confidence, you will continue to succeed. What a wonderful cycle! A great attitude, the courage to venture, and a positive belief system will ultimately lead to increased self-confidence.

Let me share a story of when I was acting in a movie in Northern California and the character I was portraying was a surfer. The studio had hired a world champion wave rider to be my coach. Being a country boy from East Texas, the closest I had ever come to surfing was standing up on a sled being pulled by a mule. I got up many times successfully during rehearsal. Then, when the director called "Action!" I paddled fast and caught a wave just right, getting up with perfect balance. I was confident that I wouldn't fall because my coach was right next to me. Suddenly I realized that my coach had not caught the wave with me and I was riding on my own. Then what do you think happened? WIPEOUT! I had no confidence in my ability to balance on the surfboard without my coach there. I negotiated with my inner critic, asking him to cut me some slack and allow me to get back on the board and ride the wave. Instead of quitting, I knew that if I just kept getting up, over and over, I would eventually succeed. I did eventually catch the perfect wave and we got the shot.

Confidence, like enthusiasm, is contagious. If you radiate confidence, others will believe in you. I love the phrase, "Every day in every way, I'm getting better and better." If you keep getting back on your board and never quit, you will get better and better!

Now, let's build a positive belief system that will allow you to get back on your board and ride the wave!

Evaluating Your Beliefs

be·lief (n.)
1. Mental acceptance of and conviction in the truth, actuality, or validity of something.
2. Something believed or accepted as true.

The way in which you see and feel about yourself and the confidence you have in your abilities is the result of your beliefs. Beliefs are the emotional offspring of values. They suggest what we are and what we can be. Beliefs are guiding principles that give meaning to our lives. You have heard the statement many times, "Whether you believe you can or believe you can't, you are right." Beliefs, just as values, empower or limit. Because your beliefs create your life, it is in your best interest to explore and evaluate them carefully.

You are who you believe you are. You can recreate yourself and change your life by changing your beliefs. When we believe something, we send a congruent message to our brain, our brain accepts the message at face value, and the outcome is the result it produces. Success is not a secret; it is a system—a positive belief system.

For decades, many people struggled to climb Mt. Everest. During this time, an unbroken chain of tragedies and failures created the belief that Everest was unconquerable. On May 29, 1953, Sir Edmund Hillary and Tenzing Norgay shattered that belief and became the first men to stand atop Everest. Since their remarkable feat, many climbers have successfully reached that challenging summit. The belief in the unconquerable Everest is no longer spoken. Rather, the question of success now turns to the preparation and talent of each climber on each expedition.

Former Major League Baseball pitcher Jim Abbott provides another exciting example of how powerful belief can be in allowing us to perform beyond our "normal" physical limits. Although he had only one hand, he believed he could pitch. Before ever taking the mound in the majors, Abbott taught himself to play with his disability. He would tuck his glove under the stub of his missing hand, and in one motion release the ball and slip his pitching hand back into his glove. Despite his outstanding NCAA pitching record, many professional scouts believed it was impossible for a one-handed pitcher to play successfully in minor league baseball, let alone the majors. Abbott didn't share their belief. Within a few years of signing his first professional contract, he had established himself as a winner in Major League Baseball.

Your emotional habitat will either nourish or negate your attitude and belief system. Beliefs come from environment, events, experiences and knowledge. Like anything else, beliefs tend to change as we mature and gain experience.

Here is an exercise to help you evaluate your beliefs, positive and negative, so that you can decide which ones are holding you back, and which ones will move you forward.

BELIEF EVALUATION EXERCISE

Begin by making a list of beliefs that have enhanced your life and added to your success. Now, write down additional beliefs that have limited your development.

Here are some beliefs that enhance success:

> I love challenges and expect good results.
> New beginnings create new opportunities.
> The past does not equal the future.
> I can only succeed if I start.
> Every setback is a learning experience and step toward another positive outcome.

Just as positive beliefs can empower us to accomplish great things, limiting beliefs can produce disappointment and despair in our lives. They deny our basic goodness and value. They limit our potential for achievement, prosperity, health, and happiness. They refute our right to become the person we need to be, living the life we desire.

We must challenge the intelligence of our conscious minds to determine whether or not our limiting beliefs make sense. Limiting beliefs are often more difficult to recognize than positive beliefs. That's because many of them are accepted as unchangeable truths written in stone. Outcomes may seem to validate negative beliefs, but it is beliefs that create outcomes, not outcomes that create beliefs. What came first, the chicken or the egg?

Beliefs did!

Here are some beliefs that limit success:

> ➤ When people reject my ideas, they reject me.
> ➤ I'm no good at public speaking.
> ➤ I failed last time, so I'll probably fail again.

Garbage In = Garbage Out

Our subconscious mind, fed by everything I've just described: self-image, self-talk, self-confidence, and what we believe to be true about ourselves, makes sure we get everything we deserve.

Write down your answers to the following questions in your journal:

ACTING FOR REAL

What do you think you deserve in terms of success, relationships, love, etc.?
How do you think you deserve to be treated?
What kind of soul mate do you think you deserve?
Who do you listen to?
Who do you believe?
Who do you let program your belief system?
Whose prophecies are you acting out?

Observe what you have written in your journal. Highlight the beliefs that are holding you back from your goals. Make the commitment to change them. Now, circle the positive beliefs that are moving you towards your goals. See, hear, and feel yourself reaching those goals! I have my actors see themselves as the play ends, taking their bows and hearing the applause of the audience. They are a hit. By duplicating this exercise, you have just created the belief that you will succeed! Remember to stay possessed—the underlying state that is driving you through these processes!

Changing Your Beliefs

Your beliefs will not change unless you do something to change them. Learning what is productive and what will propel you towards your goals must be a higher priority for you than simply holding onto a belief for a sense of security. If you need to change an erroneous or damaging belief, you will change it. The time may vary, and there may need to be an emotional release, but with persistence, change is inevitable.

Any time you change, you must change some habits. We all have habits. Habits are automatic behaviors. Habits are free flowing, and you don't have to think about them. If we aren't careful, passivity or aggressiveness—rather than the golden mean of assertiveness—can become habitual in our behavior. Not all habits are bad. Examples of some good habits are brushing your teeth, exercise, and eating healthy food. These habits free up our minds to concentrate on other things. Bad habits taunt our minds and our subconscious because we struggle with knowing that we can and should do better. Habits, in and of themselves, allow us to do many things at once without having to think too much. We have the power to put this ability to use by developing positive habits. Our goal is to create good, assertive behavioral habits so that the behaviors we need to portray become easy, automatic, and enjoyable. We do this by establishing a positive belief system. And in doing this, we initiate change.

The first step in building a good belief system is to identify and eliminate your negative beliefs and attitudes. To change a limiting belief, you must become aware that it is running your life. You must uncover your blind spots. You must look at situations you don't care to look at. You must confront yourself with that which you would rather not confront. Your coach, friends, and family members can act as your third eye, helping you to identify the negative beliefs that are holding you back. Ask them what they would change about you if they had the chance. Now, using that information, think of something that you need to change in your life. Then make a list of the reasons why you haven't made the change already. Confronting this list will show you which reasons for not changing are valid and which are excuses. Eliminate the excuses that feed your negative beliefs. By doing so, you can make changes that will have a positive impact on your attitude and belief system. Accepting the reality that negative beliefs exist in your mind is 50% of improving your attitude and belief system.

Next, make a list of things that bring you joy in life. Joy is defined as "intense and especially ecstatic or exultant happiness." Make an effort to do at least one of the things on your list once a week. You can portray joy through physical behavior by smiling, dancing, singing, jumping up and down, laughing, and throwing your arms in the air. I love Walter Huston's dance in *The Treasures of the Sierra Madre*. When he realized that they had struck gold, he was ecstatic! He revealed pure joy. That is a great movie to observe and then model ecstatic and exultant happiness. By taking these steps to bring joy into your life, you will be contributing to a great attitude and a belief system based on joy and optimism.

Another step towards a great attitude is to identify positive examples using an acting exercise that I've created called the "Picture Exercise."

PICTURE EXERCISE

Find a magazine or newspaper picture in which a person is revealing a great attitude—a picture of optimism.

Now duplicate that picture (costume, pose, mood, etc.) and freeze until you get a sense of the emotion. Hold on to that emotion.

Post the picture up somewhere and walk, talk, and move the way that person would, using your own humanitarian causes. You are now creating the psychological gesture of the person in that picture and connecting it to your own internal emotions!

If you act like the people you admire, you will begin to take on their traits. Surround yourself with positive, optimistic people with great attitudes because it creates the atmosphere you need in order to achieve your own positive results. Model the best to be the best!

Now, remember a time in your life when you busted out of a comfort zone that disproved a negative belief, such as when you moved away from home. Did you think that you weren't going to survive in the cold cruel world? Were you scared that you weren't going to make it? What happened? You became stronger, wiser, and more self-sufficient as a result. Busting out of your comfort zone resulted in a positive outcome!

Another way of changing self-limiting beliefs is by having an empowering, metaphorical experience that, although targeted at a specific belief, is intense enough to cause you to challenge a broad range of limiting beliefs. For example, the experience of walking on hot coals without sustaining any burns causes a person to challenge the strongly held belief that to walk on hot coals always results in burns. This "walking on fire" experience serves as a metaphor to challenge many other limiting beliefs and would immediately cause you to ask yourself, "If I can do this when I thought this was impossible, how many other things can I really do?" This powerful, metaphorical experience changes clusters of limiting beliefs just like a cue ball shatters the "rack" in a game of pool. The ability to place yourself in a possessed state that empowers you to do things that you previously thought impossible is a key learning process for you, the Actor for Real.

When acting, it always astounded me how I was able to go beyond my own capabilities and self-limiting belief systems by portraying characters that stretched my comfort zone and changed my beliefs about what was possible, on the screen and in my life. By believing in the character that I had created, I could accomplish any great physical, emotional, or psychological feat. Think of all the movies you've seen where actors have gone beyond their own physical capabilities to create a character. Great actors constantly challenge their belief system and bust out of their comfort zones to create full dimensional characters. In revealing the behavior of your character, you will find that you, the Actor for Real, can achieve extraordinary results in your life by supporting the belief system that anything is possible.

Holding fast to your belief that anything is possible, use imagined experience to project into your mind the accomplishment of an objective that directly challenges a limiting belief you hold. This process is called *outcome management* and is a strategy for developing a belief system based on the world the way you desire it to be. Choose an outcome that you are aiming for, but is currently blocked by a limiting belief. Now, imagine yourself reaching that goal. See it, hear it, taste it, smell it and feel it. Imagine with certainty the feelings that would attend such a success. Notice how your life would be different, what people would say, what you would think and what you would see. Your brain does not know the difference between the world outside your body and the world that is projected onto the screen in your mind. The mind accepts the imagined experience as true. This method is as effective as actual external performance. This process is all about change and success using strategies that facilitate your outcomes.

The first step of any process is to start. On a movie set, when the actors are ready, the director yells, "ACTION!" Just like on the stage and screen, action is life's only command. Action is the experience we have when we are fully present and focused in the moment. It is the movement and activity stemming from the natural creative energy that flows through every living thing and is the source of our vitality. The simple action of moving forward in your life towards your goals will cause an immediate change in attitude. If you have a great attitude, you can get started. Taking action will trigger a new empowered belief that you can reach your positive outcomes, thus creating a new belief system.

Start! That's the key. If you don't start, you will never achieve success. Once you do start, the whole universe works with you.

ACTING FOR REAL

This is the immutable principle of cause and effect. Nike's phenomenal marketing campaign is based on this premise: "Just do it."

One of the truest statements ever made is, "A successful person does what unsuccessful people are unwilling to do." There is no magical get-rich-quick formula. You have to do it!

Validate yourself for each action, no matter how small, that you take towards your goals. Reward yourself for your everyday wins and accomplishments. Encourage and validate the conflict within yourself—from conflict comes growth. In acting, if there is no conflict, there is no scene. Just like in life, if there is no struggle to overcome a challenge, there is no change. Every action produces an outcome, just like every outcome produces a new action. There are no failures, only outcomes. Remember to be patient because real change takes time. And lastly, don't quit!

Here's an example to illustrate the power of a positive belief system and great attitude:

Bruce Dern and I have been friends for many years. In addition to being a great actor, and the father of Laura Dern, he is also a marathon runner. I used to go to his races with him and for the last three to five miles I would run alongside him and keep him focused on his belief that he could finish the race.

Somewhere during the last two to three miles of races, runners "hit the wall"—they go into a mental *Twilight Zone* because their body has been depleted of so many natural reserves and nutrients. With this, comes their attack on their own belief system —"I can't finish" "I can't go on" and "I have to quit."

In Bruce's case, I would encourage him through "the wall," to keep his belief system intact and not let the negativity overpower his positive attitude. I would tell him not to let his attitude change from "winning" to "quitting." This is also what people do in life —they let negativity overpower their positive attitudes and belief systems. They allow their inner critics and victim characters to lose the race!

Here's another example of how strongly our belief system and attitude affects us. I was in Sydney on a consulting job in 1991 and fell in love with this particular story.

Every year, Australia hosts a 600-kilometer (373-mile) foot race from Sydney to Melbourne, a race that takes five days and makes marathons look like a jog to the corner store. As the story goes, in 1988 there was a certain unlikely athlete who showed up to run in the race. As he was filling out paperwork, everyone assumed that he was registering for another runner, not himself. After all, he was 61 years old and he wore overalls with galoshes over his work boots, just like the farmers I knew in East Texas. He showed up to join a group of over 150 world-class athletes, mostly between the ages of 18 and 25 years old.

As he shuffled away from the table in his galoshes and pinned number 64 to his overalls, it became evident to everybody that he was actually going to run.

ACTING FOR REAL

They all said, "This must be a publicity stunt. There's no way this is for real. He'll be down in 30 minutes," and they laughed at him.

The curious press shoved their microphones into number 64's face:

Press: "Who are you?"

Number 64: "I'm Cliff Young and I'm a sheepherder."

Press: "Have you ever run in a 600-kilometer race before?"

Cliff: "Nope, this is my first."

Press: "Well, then you can't run. You'll kill yourself!"

Cliff: "Yes I can, and no I won't."

Press: "Why do you believe you can keep pace with these athletes that are less than half your age?"

Cliff: "See, I grew up on a farm where we couldn't afford horses or a motorbike so whenever the storms would roll in, I'd have to go out and round up the sheep. We had over two thousand head of sheep on a couple thousand acres of land. I know I can run this race. Five days? I've had to run sheep for three!"

When the gun went off and the race started, all the world-class athletes took off, while people shouted, "Somebody stop him, he's crazy!" All of Australia was watching this crazy old guy, shuffling along in his galoshes way in the back of the pack.

The existing paradigm for this race was to run eighteen hours and sleep six. But Cliff never stopped—he kept running. Every night he got just a little bit closer. By the last night he shuffled past the pack. By the last day he was in the lead.

Not only did Cliff Young run the Melbourne to Sydney race at age 61, all 600 kilometers of it without dying, he won first place by nine hours and became a national hero. Why did Cliff Young win? As he said himself, "I didn't know you were supposed to sleep."

His belief system was chasing sheep and trying to outrun a storm. Cliff Young, with every conceivable limitation against him, changed the whole paradigm of that race. Now, nobody sleeps and the runners use the "Cliff Young" shuffle because it's more energy efficient than the way they ran before.

If that can happen to Cliff Young in such a physically demanding race, imagine what can happen to you if you have the right belief system and a great attitude! Remember...

A+A=A

A great **ATTITUDE** + A little bit of **APTITUDE** =
all the **ALTITUDE** you desire!
You can go as high as the sky!

The final phase in the process of attaining a great attitude and enlightened state of mind includes introducing yourself in present time, affirming the confident beliefs that fuel your self-image, and setting a plan in motion for success.

ACTING FOR REAL

I Am

The first step in taking ownership of your identity is to identify the final product. Who are you?

In my acting class I have an exercise called "The Interview," in which the student walks to the center of the stage, says his name, and then tells me about himself. Most of the time he says, "My name is…" and "I'm from…" He might as well be introducing his foot, not himself.

Saying "my name is" puts you outside of yourself, away from present time. However, when you say "I am"—you are in present time, taking responsibility for your "I AM" personality. Whenever you are revealing yourself in life you must be in present time.

So do it, you will like it. You must be in present time to take action and achieve your outcomes. So, who are you? "I am the star… your name." First, are you a man, a woman or a human being? Yes, you are human. Yes, you are a being. But most important, is that you are a woman or a man. The public will follow a man or woman, but not a human being. Remember Helen Reddy's song, "I Am Woman"? And as Will Rogers said, "I never met a man I didn't like." But I'm sure he met a lot of human beings he didn't care for. You must break out of the pack, and lead—as a man, or a woman!

"I AM," similar to your identity, is about getting back to specificity.

INTERVIEW EXERCISE

Make your list:

1. I am woman.
2. I am man.
3. I am wife.
4. I am lover.
5. I am teacher.
6. I am _____.

Who are you? Write down the roles you play in life in your journal and say them out loud in front of a mirror—be possessed!

You've just learned how to introduce yourself in present time, taking responsibility for your identity. Now it's time to put your positive belief system, powerful identity and sense of "I AM" into action.

Plan for Success—you deserve it!

Suc·cess (n.)
1. The achievement of something desired, planned, or attempted.
2. A result or an outcome.

"If constructive thoughts are planted, positive outcomes will be the result. Plant the seeds of failure and failure will follow."
— *Sidney Madwed*

I can immediately tell when a student is not sincere about becoming an actor when I hear the following phrase: "Well, I really want to be an actor so I'll try it for a few years, and if I don't make it, I'll do something else." In that one statement, the student has committed to a negative outcome before he has even started. It's obvious that his belief system is weak.

On the other hand, I can just as quickly spot the student who will be a success in whatever he does in life, when he utters a significantly more powerful phrase: "I must act." If you *must* do something, your positive belief system will eliminate the chance of a negative outcome, simply because you have not allowed that option to enter into your subconscious. When you must do something, it is a need. Need is a powerful emotion that will drive you to success. Your subconscious, like your inner critic, has radar that can spot an intention, positive or negative, miles away. "Trying to do something" is a prerequisite for failure. Do it or don't do it—never try! If you must do something, there are no other options.

By spending any portion of your time worrying and therefore planning what you will do if you fall short of your goals, you are unconsciously working toward that negative outcome. A more productive use of that same energy would be to put it into the work leading to success. By anticipating the worst, you are preparing yourself to live within the problem, instead of preparing to quickly solve any challenges that you encounter on your path to success. Living within the problem is safe, comfortable, and poses few challenges or obstacles. You become used to it. Misery loves company and you have allowed the problem to be the solution. This is a trap leading to negative outcomes and you must be careful not to fall into it on the way to reaching your goals.

Therefore, when backup plans are given value, what may start as "intelligent planning" and "covering all the bases" escalates into full-fledged fear of failure that can stop all of your efforts. What was once a solid game plan with high hopes and intentions has now been sabotaged by a foundation of "what ifs." When I was a young actor, people seemed to enjoy asking me, "If you don't make it, what do you plan to fall back on?" My favorite answer for them was, "I don't fall back, I fall forward."

Take A Bow!

Congratulations! You now possess the enlightened state of mind and positive attitude necessary for all of your empowered life characters. By having a great attitude, positive belief system, self-confidence and being possessed, you have put yourself in the right state of mind to begin your training as an Actor for Real.

BALANCE
Thom horseback riding in the 1971 film
Valdez is Coming

CHAPTER 3
BOP
BALANCED

"She bop, he bop, a-we bop, I bop, you bop, a-they bop…"
—*Cyndi Lauper*

When I was a teenager, there was a dance at the time called "the be-bop," or as the adults called it, "the dirty boogie." And here I am now, all these years later, going back to my youth and back to "BOP."

Be BOP!

Bop isn't about the dirty boogie, it's about being grounded in the ultimate state of *readiness*—a solid foundation for all the greatness you will achieve in life.

BOP is the Essence of Excellence!

When in BOP, you are:

B = Balanced
O = Observant
P = Present

Have you ever wondered what athletes mean when they refer to "being in the zone"? The zone is the state where they are at the top of their game, performing flawlessly, and it is a seemingly effortless joy. How do they get into this ambiguous state of greatness—physically, psychologically, emotionally, or otherwise?

BOP is that state of greatness—balanced, observant, and present. And the good news is it's not just for athletes anymore.

45

ACTING FOR REAL

Everyone can achieve greatness by being in BOP! When you are balanced, you are on the balls of your feet, steady, and prepared for whatever life throws at you. Being observant means you're looking at life with your eyes wide open. When you are in present time, you're in the moment, the NOW.

BOP is being ready and available to the most that life has to offer you—emotionally, physically, spiritually, and mentally. Being in BOP, your sensory acuity is firing on all cylinders. By examining each component of BOP one at a time, you will learn how simple it is to attain this state of greatness.

Balance

bal·ance (n.)
1. A state of bodily equilibrium.
2. A stable mental or psychological state; emotional stability.
3. A harmonious or satisfying arrangement or proportion of parts or elements, as in a design.

The first step to being in BOP is to make sure that your feet are squarely planted on the ground and ready for action. If you are physically out of balance, the smallest of obstacles in your path will knock you off course. Being in balance means using your sensory acuity—physical and otherwise—to see where you are in relation to your surroundings. We all know the importance of balanced nutrition, balanced behavior, balanced activity, and a balanced environment. But it all begins with balancing your body physically.

How many times have you heard someone say, "Stay on your toes!" "Stand up straight!" and "Don't be caught off balance"? That's because most people go through life out of balance, which reveals the victim character.

Check the bottoms of your shoes. Is the heel more worn out than the toe? This is a sign of being perpetually out of balance. If your heel is significantly more worn, you are tilted backward, ready and waiting to be knocked down. Are you feeling out of control? Get on the balls of your feet! Don't be caught flat-footed! Get on your toes! On your mark—get ready, set, go!

When new students enter my class, I first observe the way they walk into the room. Their walk reveals how in BOP they are. If they're balanced, they are on the balls of their feet, planted about shoulder-width apart and their body is squared up, leaning forward. If they're off-balance, they walk at a tilt, stand with their legs too close together or too far apart, on their heels or on their toes, and are ready to be knocked down by anyone and anything that comes along. They have put themselves at a disadvantage before they have given themselves a chance to succeed. By being physically out of balance, they will be slow to move forward and take productive action.

An actor reveals being under the influence by duplicating the behavioral characteristics of chemical impairment. An individual who has been drinking or doing drugs will be tilted backward on his heels, fighting to regain his lost sense of balance. Just like in life when a police officer stops someone he suspects of being under the influence, he asks the person to walk a straight line. If you are out of balance in life—physically, mentally, emotionally, spiritually, or otherwise—you will appear similar to that drunk, unable to walk a straight line. You will be falling backwards in life instead of moving forward.

Like everything else that is important in life, balance requires practice. In order to perfect the concepts in this book, you will have to create a need to practice them as a scheduled part of your "work week" as an Actor for Real. You must create a need to be in BOP.

In everything you do, remember to remain balanced and suddenly, life won't be such an uphill battle. When you encounter a road bump, immediately stop what you're doing and find what has fallen out of balance in your life. Are you physically off-balance? Emotionally? Is it your diet? Is that addictive personality rearing its ugly head? Once you have identified what has thrown you off balance, use that level of awareness to make the necessary changes to get back on track.

Being balanced is the first step in being BOP—the essence of excellence! Are you ready to start? Plant your feet shoulder-width apart, square up your body, get on the balls of your feet, and lean forward…

Thom in the 1981 CBS movie *Hellinger's Law*

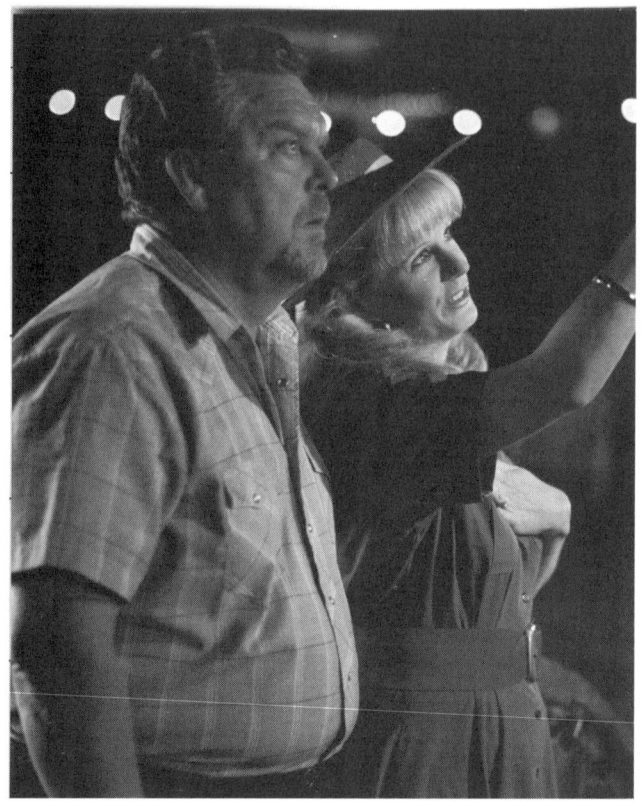

OBSERVANT

Thom with P.J. Soles in the 1997 horror classic
Uncle Sam

CHAPTER 4
BOP
OBSERVANT

Now that you are balanced and ready for action, you must be observant of yourself and your surroundings. The power of observation is one of your most important tools as an Actor for Real and the second step to being in BOP. Creative people are especially observant because they've trained themselves to value observation. Observation is your greatest teacher.

ob·ser·va·tion (n.)
1. The act or the faculties of observing or taking notice; the act of seeing, or of fixing the mind upon, anything.
2. The result of an act, or of acts, of observing; view; reflection; conclusion; judgment.

As described above, "observation" is a very comprehensive term. It incorporates many factors, including everything we perceive using our sensory acuity as well as everything we perceive instinctively, both consciously and unconsciously.

Accurate observation and mental recording count tremendously for the actor. Most people do not practice ardent observation on a regular basis. But you, the Actor for Real, must practice observation constantly in order to combine the psychology, emotional life, and behaviors necessary to create your empowered life character.

ACTING FOR REAL

We can deliberately increase our power of observation by making the choice to be more aware of ourselves and our surroundings.

Are you looking at life with eyes wide open? The observant person is interested in everything around him—the colors, images, settings, and backgrounds—everything in life. How observant are you?

OBSERVATION EXERCISE

Study an animal, any animal. Study your dog, your cat, the bird at the local pet store, a gorilla at the zoo, or your best friend's iguana. What is the animal's posture? When and how does he move? Why do you think he moves? What could he be thinking? Begin to "mirror" the animal. Move when he moves. Think like he thinks. If the animal is inactive, be inactive. Study him, be as specific as possible.

Look into the animal's eyes. Is he intelligent? Tame? Dangerous? Think as the animal. When you imitate his movements, ask yourself why you move that way. Keep the physical aspects of the animal and transform them into the human counterpart of yourself.

Notice how these behaviors and postures make you feel. Try them in public and notice how others respond to you. By personifying a lion, others may see the fire in your eyes. By personifying the postures of a gorilla, they may see heaviness, a slouched appearance, translating into defeat. Contrastingly, move through the world like a bird and notice the lightness and energy you bring into a room.

As you become more aware of behaviors, postures, gestures, and thoughts that can be seen and not heard, you will begin to have a better understanding of the world around you and how you can command your presence and master the art of guiding the responses of those around you.

Awareness

"Awareness is a state of being in which you may choose to live. It means to be awake to the moment. It is about being keenly observant about what is so, and why; about what is occurring, and why; about what can cause it not to occur, and why; about all the possible—and the most probable—outcomes of any choice or action, and what makes them possible and probable."
—*Neale Donald Walsch*

a·ware·ness (n.)
1. Having knowledge of.
2. State of elementary or undifferentiated consciousness.

An actor's awareness is one of his greatest and most important tools. When he's filming, he has to be aware of the camera, the props, other characters in the scene, his voice, his mark, the lighting and numerous other variables. Despite all these distractions, he has to deliver a natural performance. As an Actor for Real, you will see how awareness is vital to the development of your empowered character. Awareness encompasses the entire triangle of BOP.

Awareness is the degree of clarity with which we perceive and understand all factors that affect our lives. The awareness of your behavior begins through self-observation without judgment. Ask yourself, "Do I really know who I am? Do I know myself with the kind of objectivity that I can at times apply to others?"

You can greatly enhance your powers of observation by considering yourself a human research laboratory. As the song goes, "Getting to know you, getting to know all about you…" By observing your external behavior in the smallest sense, you can explore your habits and reactions and get a glimpse of yourself as others see you. Once your aim becomes self-exploration, you will find there is no adventure more exciting or more rewarding! You will enjoy being a work in progress for the rest of your life.

CASTING EXERCISE

This is an acting exercise that I created to help actors improve their awareness and powers of observation. Do this exercise in your journal.

1. Think of somebody you know well.

2. Imagine that they have just committed a heinous crime and you are the only eyewitness.

3. Write down everything you remember about him or her and describe their appearance and behavior in as much detail as possible, as if you were identifying them for the police sketch artist. Be very specific.

4. Ask a friend of the suspect to identify the person you've described in your journal. If they cannot, go back and re-evaluate the exercise with further detail. If they can, good job observing!

5. Compare this profile with the suspect the next time you see them. Which information matches and which does not? Which information was missing from the profile that you're observing now?

Here's the payoff:

Do the same exercise using yourself as the suspect and see what happens. How well do you really know yourself? Don't get lost in speculation of how you desire others to see you—it must be perfectly straightforward and objective. Describe yourself as honestly as someone else would. In order to do this successfully, you have to remove the blind spots, prejudices, and justifications that are a part of your daily life. Draw a picture of yourself so accurate that if you gave it to a police sketch artist, you'd be arrested! Now, give your profile to another person and see if they can guess whom you are describing. Ask them if they can add anything that you've missed to your profile. Then ask a few more friends to do the same. This process gives you a glimpse of how other people see you and allows you the flexibility to make positive changes in the characters that you are portraying in life.

When working with an actor, I have him sit in a chair and see the character in the scene just like he was watching a movie. It is important for him to observe the character's behavior, including habits, ticks, addictions, and imperfections, so that he may duplicate them accurately. This allows him to step into the given circumstances and then cast himself as the character. The challenge for the actor is to duplicate what he has observed as honestly as the writer and director have envisioned it. You must have the same level of awareness when creating your empowered life character, since you are the writer, director, and star in your life.

ACTING FOR REAL

Here's an example of how I got a glimpse of myself. When I had my annual physical, I sneaked a look at my chart and saw that the doctor had described me as an "obese, middle-aged male." What upset me the most is that I had never seen myself as a fat, middle-aged man. No matter how it hurt me, I knew that I could not do anything about my age, but I could do something about the obesity. Once I became observant of my body and how I really looked, I started making changes in my diet and overall health. I got a glimpse of myself and it gave me an epiphany to make necessary changes in my life.

SELF-OBSERVATION EXERCISE

John Abbott, the late, great Shakespearean character actor and acting teacher, told me that acting was observing life, reading extensively, and starting and finishing projects. Acting for Real demands the same principles. Like a painter, you're painting your self-portrait. Picasso's best portrait was of himself.

Watch Movies, TV, and Plays

If you carefully watch and question the character's behavior, actions and reactions, their attitudes and prejudices, you can heighten your powers of observation just as you can by observing and questioning the behavior of real-life individuals.

Visit Museums

Observe the artist's concept that he has captured on the canvas through color, light, and emotion. This improves your powers of observation by stimulating your creative imagination. Art feeds art.

Read Books

Read extensively! Reading strengthens your powers of observation by allowing you to observe the behavior of the characters in the book and vicariously travel to wherever it takes you.

Observe your Habitat and Lifestyle

To be observant of yourself and your essence, you need to be aware of your environment and observant of the space that you occupy. How do you live?

As an Actor for Real, you are required to be more observant than most. It is your task to see things in ways you haven't noticed before. If you're observing life with your eyes wide open, you will see a need for change, propelling you closer and closer towards your goals.

Sharpening your powers of observation will not only help you survive, but when mastered, will serve to enlighten you. BOP is one state of greatness—not three separate concepts. If you're observant, you'll know when you're off balance. Now let's learn how to be present.

You're either in BOP, or not in BOP. So…be BOP!

PRESENT

Thom in his Best Supporting Actor role for a theatrical
production in *Rainmaker* by N. Richard Nash

CHAPTER 5
BOP
PRESENT

"Right here, right now.
There is no other place I want to be..."
                                        —Jesus Jones

pres·ent
1. (n.)The here and now.
2. (v.)To be in real time.

In school, when your name was called, did you raise your hand or did you holler out "Present!" As a kid, I always thought that this was funny, because when the teacher called roll she always looked right at me! I felt that if she couldn't see me right in front of her, *she* wasn't present!

Being Present

To be present, in real time, with your attention in the here and now, is the final and most important piece of BOP. Being present gives you the ability to allow and accept people and things into your life and to comfortably occupy the same space with them. Let's explore what it is to be completely present in your everyday life as an Actor for Real.

When Bill Cosby was first starting out as a stand-up comic, he was booked at a top nightclub in Chicago. As the story goes, it was a tough room to work and he went from being extremely nervous to completely frozen with fear—he bombed!

ACTING FOR REAL

When he left the stage, he immediately ran up to the club owner and said, "I'm sorry. I was terrible. In fact, I was so bad that you don't even have to pay me!"

The club owner grabbed him by his lapels, got right in his face, and said, "You're damn right I don't have to pay you! You're the worst comedian I've ever booked! You were terrible! I never want to see you again! Get out of town!"

As Bill Cosby was slinking away, the owner added, "And by the way, would you stop over at the hotel and send that funny young comedian over to do the rest of your shows?" Cosby looked at the owner and said, "Which young comedian?" And the owner said, "The real Bill Cosby!"

That wise old club owner knew that Bill Cosby had listened to his inner critic, who was telling him he wasn't ready yet, the room was too big, and that he wasn't funny enough. Listening to his inner dialogue and negative self-talk had taken him out of present time.

When Bill Cosby came back to do his act he was in present time, making each moment real, and playing off the audience. He was a hit!

Now let's explore how to be present by consciously tuning your sensory acuity, being *real now*, and focusing your attention in present time. Because not everyone in life will give you a second chance to get it right, like that club owner did for Bill Cosby.

Sensory Acuity

sen·so·ry a·cu·i·ty (n.)
1. Acuteness of sensory perception.
2. Keenness of sight, hearing, feeling, taste, and smell.

This simple and fun exercise will help you get into present time. Get out your journal and tune your sensory acuity into the here and now. Record everything that you're taking in right now through your senses:

SENSORY EXERCISE

What do you see?
What do you feel?
What do you hear?
What do you taste?
What do you smell?

You will enhance this exercise even more by repeating it. Have fun with it! The more consciously you do it, the more attuned your sensory acuity will be. You will be focused, in present time, and in BOP!

Real Now

Tuning your sensory acuity places you in present time by making you aware of your physical environment. Being *real now* requires a conscious awareness and understanding of the impulses that determine your actions within that environment.

ACTING FOR REAL

To be *real now* means that you have to check yourself—ask yourself some basic questions to get rooted in the present and be real, *now*! This is a self-check system rooted into the creative ground that will sow positive outcomes by putting you in real time.

FOUR PILLARS OF CREATION & CHARACTERIZATION EXERCISE

This is an exercise that I created to coach actors on how to develop characters and portray them in present time. It creates a link, so that the actor directs the character instead of vice versa. When an actor creates a character, he uses the following questions to stimulate his imagination so that he will always be in present time. The Four Pillars brings actors out of the fog and back into the here and now, in control of their performance. This is the same process that you can use to connect with the characters you portray in life.

Write down your answers to these questions.

I. Who am I?

Asking yourself this question stimulates your imagination and makes you focused, in charge, and responsible for your outcomes.

—"I AM" Thom McFadden, coach, father, husband, actor, writer, mentor, director, man.

II. Where am I?

In order to locate your exact position in time and space, take yourself off autopilot and gain control of your actions, ask yourself—Where am I? This allows you to intellectually make choices and understand where you are in present time.

Where's the location? What's the atmosphere? What am I doing?

—"I AM" at home, in my office, at my desk, sitting in my chair, on a bright sunny day, typing on the computer.

—I see my fingers typing, I hear the sounds of the keyboard, I feel the cool breeze coming in the window, I smell the fresh cut grass outside my window, I taste my coffee.

III. Who am I with?

You then ask—Who am I with? This places your attention in present time—on yourself, with a loved one, in a crowd, etc. It identifies which of your "I AM" personalities is the right one to reveal.

What is my connection with this person? What do I need from him? What is my outcome?

—"I AM" with a client, I am his coach, I need him to learn, I desire him to be empowered.

What if "I AM" alone with myself? I ask myself these questions:

Do I have the right attitude?
Am I responsible for my outcomes?
Am I being driven by a positive, empowering belief system?
Am I awake?
Am I in present time?

IV. How do I feel?

And finally, you ask—How do I feel? Am I ready for action? Where will these feelings take me on my course of action? Am I committed?

ACTING FOR REAL

Until you are, there is hesitancy, holding back, and ineffectiveness concerning acts of initiative and creation. The moment you commit yourself with certainty, the universe moves with you.

In assessing how you feel in the here and now, you are addressing your present needs and desires, the best indicators of your overall state. When examined honestly, this tells you more about yourself than any other area and gives you insight as to whether your answers to the other three questions were truthful.

Your emotional reactions (the way you feel) will be most revealing if you take the time and effort to honestly examine them. Get in touch with yourself by recognizing and accepting the reality of your emotions!

What state of emotion am I in?
—"I AM" excited, nervous, sad, happy, possessed, etc.

The "Four Pillars" exercise is a process of checks and balances that puts you in real time—NOW!

Attention

"For consciousness, attention is necessary. Attention is as oil in the lamp. Consciousness is the light"
                                        —Madame Ouspensky

at·ten·tion (n.)
1. Concentration of the mental powers upon an object; a close or careful observing or listening.
2. The ability or power to concentrate mentally.
3. A readiness to respond to stimuli.

con·scious·ness (n.)
   1. Immediate knowledge or perception of the presence of any object, state, or sensation.
   2. An alert cognitive state in which you are aware of yourself and your situation.

Consciousness is the light that illuminates your concentration. It is turned on by your attention, which results in your outcomes. Consciousness is a skill that must be learned and continuously tuned, rather than an innate body function whose existence is taken for granted.

In *Joyful Wisdom*, Friederich Nietzsche wrote:

> Consciousness is regarded as a fixed given magnitude! Its growth and intermittences are denied. It is accepted as the unity of the organism. This ludicrous over-valuation and misconception of consciousness has, as a result, the great utility that a too-rapid maturing of it has been hindered. Because men believe that they already possess consciousness, they give themselves very little trouble to acquire it.

An actor must be aware of how he functions, since he does not have the luxury of walking around in a wakeful sleep as many others do. He has to be in a conscious state of self-awareness in order to portray his characters in present time.

When you're in present time your attention is completely focused. There is a connection, an energy force, and a heat, just like a laser beam. As an actor, or an Actor for Real, focusing your attention is the most important skill that you will learn. When acting in a movie, the actor must be in present time, "in the moment," because there are tremendous distractions all around him. There are people walking into his line of vision (his "sight line"), microphones hanging over his head, hot lights on him, off-stage noises, and things falling. If anything can go awry, it usually does. Everyone on the set is watching him do his job. On top of all that, the actor may be revealing heartfelt emotions, yet performing them to the camera instead of to another actor.

As the story goes, when shooting the famous taxi scene in the movie *On the Waterfront*, Marlon Brando's dialogue was filmed first. When it came time for Rod Steiger's close-up, Brando had already left for the day and Rod was left to deliver his emotional, heartfelt monologue to the script girl. If Mr. Steiger's attention had not been completely focused, his performance would have suffered. Instead, he was nominated for an Academy Award.

Just like in acting, if your concentration is not crystallized you will lose your objectives in the scenes that play out in your life. If you're not in present time, "in the moment," the character you're portraying will suffer, because at that moment you have become vulnerable (open for attack). Your attention has been drawn to something else and you are no longer in charge, so your concentration scrambles to pick up the pieces and get back on course.

Attention penetrates the very strata of energy. It helps to nourish and centralize the mental processes. Attention draws a stream of physical energy to produce results, the same way a magnifying glass centralizes heat rays from the sun. Attention collects the forces, knowledge, sensations and feelings, like a mirror collects light. Then focus becomes crystallized toward one objective.

When I go to a screening of a movie with the cast and crew, guess where their attention is? Wardrobe is looking at the costumes. The set designer is looking at the sets. The sound department is tuned in to the sound. The editor is watching how the audience responds to his cuts. The cinematographer is observing the lighting and photography. The writer is listening to see if his story is being told. The director is watching the big picture, the producer is counting the receipts, and the actor is watching his performance. Everyone's attention is crystallized on his or her finished product.

Present Time

If you're in present time it means that your sensory acuity is in tune, you're listening, you're observant, and you're in BOP. What if you are not present? Are you living in the past? Or are you so far out in the future that you're nowhere near the here and now? Is this you?

You know these types: looking over your shoulder during conversation, talking at their feet, interrupting you in mid-sentence, laughing at the sky, or pontificating for the simple reason to hear themselves speak. You get the feeling that your presence isn't even required! You're in a conversation with a recording. When you talk to them, you can see that the bank windows are closed. I've noticed actors do this in meetings and casting interviews, time and time again. They've lost the ability to communicate effectively because they're not in present time. Actors are constantly told to be "in the moment" and "present." How do you know when you are present?

You are present when:

    You are aware of what you are receiving via your senses.
    You are aware of everything that is influencing you right now.
    Your attention is focused consciously on self-observation.
    You are in a constant state of self-awareness.

That's how you know!

I can tell whether or not a student is in present time by the way he rehearses a scene. The actor who is present demonstrates the first two behaviors of BOP—he is in physical balance and acutely observant of everything around him. Being present means that his sensory acuity is intact and his instrument is in tune. His creative imagination soars, as evidenced by his flexibility of acting choices. As in life, acting scenes rarely unfold according to plan, despite long periods of rehearsal. When new, unrehearsed circumstances or dialogue are thrown at the actor who is in present time, he catches them and incorporates them into the scene. The actor is connected to his audience by an energy force—100 percent of his light is focused in the here and now. Whether in an acting scene or in real life, all of the above facets of being present are necessary.

Every type of human intention and meaning that exists within the universe is important. When you are in present time, you have the capacity to receive these signals. Now you are open and accessible in each moment to whatever may or may not happen, without looking to the past and comparing it to what you had hoped would happen, and without looking to the future to the possible consequences of what may or may not happen.

Be present in this moment because this moment will never happen again—it's history!

Balance is the ability to manage the sometimes conflicting demands of work and personal life. How much balance do you feel is present in your life? A lack of balance leaves many people feeling over-stressed and unfulfilled.

The power to be observant reveals what is around you and allows you to look at life with your eyes wide open.

Being present lets you hear yourself, listen to others, and be a part of what is happening NOW!

BOP allows you to move forward and be productive in your life.

BOP is three individual states working together to achieve one magnificent state of human excellence. To be BOP you must be balanced, observant, and present. Achieving only one or two of the states of BOP is useless—it's all or nothing! Being balanced and observant are fruitless states if your head is somewhere else—yesterday's upsetting phone call, tomorrow's power meeting, or simply drifting aimlessly through daydreams. You cannot be BOP if you are not in the moment. Just as you cannot be balanced if you are not observant, you cannot observe if you are not in balance, and so forth. BOP is an intricate machine, requiring its three powerful components to work together in exact synchronicity for it to work at all. To be in control of this machine, you need to be consciously aware of who's running it.

Joy and happiness are the indicators of BOP in a human machine…

An inner joyousness, amounting to ecstasy, is the normal condition of the genius mind. And lack of that joyousness develops body-destroying toxins. That inner ecstasy of the mind is the secret fountain of perpetual youth and strength in any man. He who finds it finds omnipotence and omniscience. That's BOP!

CHAPTER 6
WHO ARE YOU AND WHO DO YOU INTEND TO BE?

"It's not who you are that holds you back, it's who you think you're not."

—Unknown

Michelangelo, when asked how he sculpted *David*, answered, "I just chipped away all the marble that did not look like a man." In a similar way we can, perhaps, find our real selves by chipping away what is not truly us. Let us explore the possibilities so that we may understand the fundamental principles of who we are, using this process of self-discovery.

Am I my actions?
No, I am not my actions. I am that which acts. My actions are the means I choose to fulfill my outcomes.

Am I my body?
No, I am not my body. My body is merely the instrument through which I function.

Am I my mind?
No, I am not my mind. For my mind is but a human computer, that receives the data of my five senses. My mind is the instrument through which my awareness functions.

Am I my awareness?
No, I am not my awareness. I am that which is aware. My awareness is the sum of my life experiences, for I function through my awareness.

Then what am I?

ACTING FOR REAL

I am a man or a woman—a unique being who portrays many roles in life. My external behaviors are connected to my internal psychology through my powers of awareness, guided by the process of self-exploration. I am a work in progress.

Self-Exploration

self ex·plo·ra·tion (n.)
1. A systematic consideration of one's own spiritual or intellectual capacities.
2. To investigate systematically; examine oneself.

You are a work in progress and will be until the day you die. That is the journey of life: mining your mind until the end. What is mind? Mind is a force, a tool through which your intellectual and emotional centers can communicate with your will. To work on oneself, you must be in constant communication with your mind. Through self-exploration, hopefully you will find the joy and excitement of constantly working on yourself to attain enlightenment. You will need finer tools and instruments to reach this state of being. You will need a different approach.

"Problems cannot be solved at the same level of awareness that created them."
—Albert Einstein

You must start by asking yourself questions. Questions are the lifeblood of self-exploration. Real questions arise from a deep need and inner search. These questions should be practical so they can lead to useful answers and new beginnings toward your inner growth and self-exploration. Be naive with your questions. Ask yourself questions with attainable answers that result from a little inner searching. Instead of, "Why am I here?" ask, "What steps am I taking right now that will move me towards my goals?" Start with smaller, practical questions that have easily recognizable answers, and put them into practice now. The answers to your questions are the solutions to your problems.

You must recognize the need to work on yourself. This is a precondition and a work in and of itself. You must realize that you are in question. You must be working on yourself all the time. When working on an acting role, the actor must ask himself questions. In self-exploration, you must do the same.

The ordinary person must work on himself daily, if the possibility is to exist for that person, to become a conscious, transformed being. By observing yourself, you can see over and over again that you are in a mechanical state. How then do you begin to turn off the autopilot? The first requirement for self-exploration is to question everything and to draw your own conclusions, based on your observations.

The second requirement for self-exploration is to stop criticizing and blaming yourself, regardless of what undesired characteristics or motivations you discover—and there will be some. No matter what obstacles you encounter, you must proceed with your inner search. When you become aware that you have done the best you could with the tools you have had to work with, regardless of your mistakes, you can discover how and why you act and react as you do. Only then can you make meaningful progress in expanding your awareness.

The third requirement for self-exploration is to maintain an active awareness of yourself and your surroundings. To really see how incomplete you are, how you drift from one direction to the other, brings the recognition that you must work on yourself. This very important condition for starting your process of self-exploration requires seriousness, honesty, and a possessed state to drive you.

SELF-EXPLORATION EXERCISE

With self-exploration, we can see ourselves as others see us. This exercise is a tool to gain awareness of yourself and will serve as a guide in your self-exploration. When working with actors on creating a role, I encourage them to use the following process of exploration in order to fully develop a character. The process of self-exploration is the same for you, the Actor for Real.

Observe, question, and think about each of the following areas of self-exploration. Then, draw your own conclusions based on your observations.

Explore the following:

1. Your Thoughts and Mental Pictures:
All actions are preceded by a thought and a picture, conscious or not. Once you become aware of the thoughts and pictures that drive your actions, you will be in greater control of your outcomes.

2. Your Triggers:
What are the belief systems behind your thoughts and mental pictures? What triggered your thoughts and where are they leading you?

3. Your Speech:
Everything you say is significant, probably much more than you realize. Be observant of what you say. Ask yourself, "Why did I say that?" Was it to request or share information? Was it to express or elicit an emotion? Was it to feed your inner critic or be critical of others? In other words, what is the need behind everything you say? Examine everything you say honestly and carefully, without judgment.

4. Your Needs, Desires and Objectives:
Your needs, desires, objectives and their implications can perhaps tell you more about yourself than any other area. Are they valid? Are they distorted? Are they constructive or destructive?

5. Your Emotional Reactions:
Your emotional reactions can be most revealing if you will take the time and effort to examine them without bias or judgment.

6. Your Addictions:
All compulsive actions are indicative of a cycle of habitual behavior that can be broken by awareness and self-observation. Ask yourself—Why am I compulsive about this? What specific emotion is responsible for this compulsive action (i.e., smoking, overeating)?

7. Your Wishes:
Explore your wishes by asking yourself—What are the needs behind my wishes? What actions have I taken towards making my wishes a reality? What actions will I take today? Make a 30-day plan. Positive outcomes are wishes brought to fruition through a great attitude and ACTION!

ACTING FOR REAL

Certainly, the more we strive to explore and understand the characters we play, the greater our awareness of human behavior will be. Once you become seriously involved in self-exploration, you will find there are no adventures more exciting and more rewarding! You will never become bored if you maintain an active interest in self-discovery. Because you are creating the character that is the STAR of your life!

Essence and Personality

es·sence (n.)
1. The real being, divested of all logical accidents.
2. That quality which constitutes or marks the true nature of anything; distinctive character; hence, virtue or quality of a thing, separated from its grosser parts.

per·son·al·i·ty (n.)
1. The totality of qualities and traits, as of character or behavior, that are peculiar to a specific person.
2. The pattern of collective characters, behavioral, temperamental, emotional, and mental traits of a person.

What did Shakespeare mean when he said, "We are all actors and the world is a stage"? Most people believe that acting is phony. They don't realize that every day they're acting out various characters in life. It is difficult to see our real self without a thorough process of self-exploration. Growth, in essence, is always the result of understanding and self-exploration. What is the "self" that we are exploring? By "self" we mean essence—the core of our being. Essence is innate, what is real and one's own. The "I AM" personalities that you now portray may not resemble your own true essence, but instead what you have acquired and learned throughout your life. In that sense, personality is not one's own. It is entirely shaped by the external world and put into motion by the driving action of the given circumstances. It's acting! This proves to me, that we are all actors playing different roles every day.

In most of us, personality is active and essence is passive. Personality determines our values, beliefs, philosophy, religion, etc. Personality, not essence, is the driving force of creativity behind the arts. Changing your personality will not change your life—but changing your essence will. Essence is the truth in a human and develops into one's individuality. The goal is to get into neutral, where essence and personality coexist!

Most of us are lacking the knowledge and understanding to use our personality to achieve our goals. By tapping into our essence, however, we gain insight into the innate components of our self, and with such insight comes a practical understanding of how to incorporate that which is truly our essence into an empowered personality. The empowered personality that results is, therefore, based upon the most powerful and organic element of our being—our essence. When you discover, through the process of self-exploration, your essence, you have discovered the genuine foundation of your Acting for Real character.

ACTING FOR REAL

Source Point

An actor's source point is his creative essence, the well from which he draws his artistic juices that stimulate his imagination. Source point is the tool of knowledge that you can use to tap into your essence. An actor, as well as an Actor for Real, must discover his own source point through the process of self-exploration in order to fully portray each of his characters behaviors. Once he finds his source point, he will be able to use it as the core of his creative process and all the characters he creates.

When revealed in a behavior in the given circumstances, it should feel natural because it's happening in the moment. A source point is a life in itself. An Actor for Real should be able to call upon it as a skill to tap into his essence and find what he needs to deepen the connection to the behavior he is portraying.

As an Actor for Real, you must discover the source point of the characters that you are portraying in life in order to develop the essence of your new empowered characters, and of yourself. An actor needs to understand where the bottom of his character is, because there lies the truth of his essence. Similarly, when creating your empowered character, it is better to work from the bottom up. Essence connects to the part being played by means of personality. This method creates a checks and balances system originating from your essence and allows you to create an enlightened personality based on the truth of who you are.

THREE WINS EXERCISE

The Three Wins exercise is recollecting your past, the key to discovering your source point. By playing the films of your past, you will achieve the wins of your future. Live in the future today by rolling back time as far as you can remember.

Remember a time in your life when you accomplished a great feat—an extraordinary win! For example: learning to ride a bicycle, your first award, the first time you won a race. Repeat this process for two other wins. These three wins are the first snapshots of your essence. Now, put those pictures together into a film. As you create your empowered personality, these films of your past will give you more and more understanding and control over the process. Your past productions will allow you to see yourself today, and are a pivotal point in your ongoing process of self-exploration.

INC. YOURSELF EXERCISE

•Be the CEO of your own make-believe company, name it, and then hire yourself.

•What is your mission statement? What is your vision down the road? What areas of your life do you wish to make changes in? How do you see yourself in six months? One year? Five years?

•What are your core values? What do you need to change in you? (What needs changing? Layoffs? Firings? If you fire yourself three times, make it a hostile takeover!)

ACTING FOR REAL

•Draw up an employment contract with yourself.

- You're the CEO!
- You're in charge of research and development!
- You're the product!
- If you don't show up for work or get the job done, fire yourself!

This process will make changes for you fast, but only if you visualize what you need to change. The clearer the outcomes, the faster and more definitive the changes will be! Ready, Set, Action!

Thom as a youth, sailing

CHAPTER 7
THE ACTOR FOR REAL

"Acting is a question of absorbing other people's personalities and adding some of your own experience."
                                    —*Paul Newman*

Acting for Real

The foundation of a positive belief system is this: we are all actors governed by different behaviors. It's not which role in life you've been cast that is important; it's how you play it. Like in the movies, some actors are bad, some are good, and some are superstars. We all have the ability to star in our own life!

The legendary football coach Knute Rockne would start his training camp by holding up a football and saying, "This is a football." Like Knute, let's start with the basics.

When I work with actors, I first explain to them what acting is. Acting is turning the psychology of a character into physical behavior. All behavior is externally based, rooted in mime, modeling, physical gesture, and other forms of nonverbal communication. Added to these is the joy experienced and release gained through some form of emotional life. Emotion is the fire that drives you to take action, whether positive or negative.

Acting is not an imitation of life.
It has a life of its own.

act·ing (v.)
1. Functioning (what life is).
2. Temporarily taking over the duties of (role-playing).
3. Behaving (performing).
4. Doing something (action).
5. Behaving in a certain way that expresses emotion (revealing).

The fundamentals of acting are accomplished by using a supposition called the "magic if." Just as in life, you "suppose" what would happen if you were placed in a certain situation. How would you act in the given circumstances?

"At the level of Imagination, the actor has the capacity to imagine him or herself in a fictional situation and allow the consequences to flow through. This occurs through the evocation of the 'magic if', a very important concept in the system."
—*Konstantin Stanislavski*

The "magic if" is a supposition that acts as a lure, allowing the actor's imagination to trick the mind into believing a set of given circumstances to be a game. Meaning, what would you do in the supposed situation? The "magic if" refers to the simple mental process of placing you, the Actor for Real, in the immediate given circumstances of the character that you are portraying. This supposition will trick your mind and allow your imagination to soar!

If an actor is called upon to represent a brutal murderer, he cannot accurately portray the emotions of that character unless he really feels them, and he cannot really feel them unless he first murders. Yet through the use of supposition, the actor is capable of duplicating those intense feelings without having murdered. The "magic if" becomes the ultimate way of freeing his imagination to portray the role.

The "magic if" is only useful if you can honestly place yourself, through your imagination, in the shoes of the character that you are portraying. Imagination is an important tool for the Actor for Real because it empowers you with new energy and vitality. It gives you many options to see things differently than you ever saw them before, and allows you to solve problems and resolve conflicts creatively before you find yourself in the actual situation.

Suppose you have a big proposal in the morning. You are trying to make a deal with a big prospective client. See yourself in the meeting. Feel enthusiastic. Hear the questions the client asks. Respond by answering the questions. See yourself bringing lightness and ease to the room. Model your behavior after someone you admire and know can get the job done. By using the "magic if," you are able to see yourself in real situations and repeat the behavior when the situation becomes real. Focus equals forecast. See yourself getting the deal and watch as your supposition turns into a reality!

Our imagination, when used correctly, is the most potent force we can employ. There is no limit as to what creative imagination can achieve for you. The imagination conceives and evokes all the emotional sensations and reactions of a particular character, which are to be revealed in the given circumstances. Nearly all acting is the result of the performer's ability to imagine and reproduce the reality of the given circumstances on the stage or screen. What actors really mean when they talk of real feeling is imagined feeling. In this sense the "magic if" is nothing more than a supposition.

Acting is a game of psychology. Half of it is understanding the psychology of human behavior. Once you have done this, you can use your imagination and the supposition "magic if" to translate that psychology into physical behavior. What the actor does is reveal to the minds and souls of his audience the workings and experiences of an assumed personality. As an Actor for Real, you will now discover how your empowered attitude, positive belief system, and understanding of the psychology of behavior are duplicated through physical actions.

Mime

Mime is the expression of thoughts and emotions through bodily actions and behavior. It is imitating through physical gestures anything that fires your imagination! This is essentially the basis of the art and craft of acting. Mime is the universal language for duplicating and revealing behavior. It is the language that binds people together through the universality of its signs and symbols. There is no true pantomime unless thought, emotion, and characteristics are blended into one perfect action. Style, manner, and form must be carefully studied, however, before mime becomes an art. The technique is only a means to an end and is not the vital part of the action. Although the body should be made free for use and the nerves and muscles properly tuned to be played upon, the subjective mind must take the lead. Acting, in the broadest sense, is always governed and guided by intelligence.

ACTING FOR REAL

The world's greatest mime is Marcel Marceau. As a style pantomime, Marceau has been acknowledged without peer. His silent exercises, which include such classic works as "The Cage," "Walking Against the Wind," "The Mask Maker," and "In The Park," as well as satires on everything from sculptors to matadors, have been described as works of genius. Of his summation of the ages of man in the famous "Youth, Maturity, Old Age and Death," one critic said, "He accomplishes in less than two minutes what most novelists can not do in volumes." As a young apprentice actor, I once had the great fortune of stage-managing Marceau when he was starring in his one-man show at UCLA. I was in awe of how he revealed the emotional life and psychology of his "Pip" character through mime.

Research has found that the average adult in our culture spends only about 25 minutes a day in articulated speech. All the rest of the time he spends communicating with others (including those all-important pauses between words) is done by nonverbal means—mime. The eye is five times more efficient than the ear in terms of the amount and specificity of the information it can collect. That is one of the reasons that it's easier to mime or duplicate behavior that you observe, than sounds that you hear.

Pantomime is the universal language because it is understood by children before they know the meaning of words. Every individual is born with the instinct to create and live in a world of imagination. Therein lies the tendency to imitate, and the desire for self-expression. These are natural, universal tendencies beginning at birth. A baby mimes before he can crawl or talk. When you're in a foreign country and don't speak the language, you mime what you need to communicate. Many romances have started when neither person spoke the other's native tongue, but were able to communicate through mime. When recounting a funny incident to your friends, using mime brings it to life. Every day you express yourself through gestures. Pantomime is the language that binds men together into one common brotherhood through the universality of its signs. Self-expression is a fundamental tool for interpreting the psychology of a character through physical behavior.

Do you remember a time when you were in a situation with someone who spoke a different language than you? Gestures transcend language barriers. Gestures, or different hand movements, are the universal language. Words are very low on the list. They are not the most important part of communication; behavior is. Behavior is expressed through mime. Mime is the root of all communication, going back to the Stone Age. It's a frequency or a vibration. In the '60s, one would say, "He had a good vibe." You get that "vibe" through gesture, behavior.

Similarly, parents communicate to their children through hand gesture. A child understands sign language so much faster than the spoken word that a trend has been set in motion to teach it to toddlers who have not yet developed speech skills.

Men and women communicate attraction to one another through flirtatious gesture. She tilts her head and twirls her hair revealing her sexuality; he smiles and puts his hand on the small of her back to show his masculine prowess. A 25-degree shift in body language demonstrates these sexual behaviors.

Alternately, power is communicated with a stance—squared up, leaning forward—asking for options and giving none. Interest in what another is saying is communicated by leaning in and giving eye contact. Watch in a restaurant. Be observant. Observe the frequency of those around you and how they relate to one another. Notice those who have trust and rapport. When he lifts his glass, she lifts hers. When she leans in, he leans forward. They mirror one another. In the same way, you will notice how other pairs are very distant, or still gauging one another, by their physical remoteness and opposing movements.

The actor is an interpretative artist—balanced, observant, and present—in BOP! It is his job to reveal the very best performance and to be able to duplicate it with the same precision expected of the pianist, flutist, violinist, ballet dancer, and any other artist. The actor's reward lies in the consciousness that he is achieving the best interpretation of human behavior. To be able to duplicate our best performance as an Actor for Real, using mime is the heart of interpretation and the ultimate goal. Be aware of your own body behavior when you are in a given situation. Make sure you are not conveying the wrong message. Change your behavior to reflect what it is you crave others to see.

In 1969, I acted in a movie starring Burt Lancaster. Most of Burt's acting was physically mimed. Observing his physical behavior and gestures, it came as no surprise to me that he was a former circus performer. He was a master of duplicating behavior, picked up through his physical performances in the circus, as well as by observing the behaviors of others and learning to mime them. He was able to communicate with the audience by revealing his universal sign language along with his killer smile!

Acting, like all arts, is symbolical. In acting, the object must be expression revealed through recognizable behavior. The actor must not merely reveal what would be natural for him to do, but instead what behavior would be symbolic of the emotions of his character. He must then reveal those things (not conceal them) by miming recognizable behavior. For example, to reveal anger, an actor might hold his breath, grit his teeth and clench his fists, duplicating symbolic behaviors of anger.

My first cousin Fred didn't talk until he was around five years old. My Aunt Gladys, his mother, eventually asked him why. He said that he didn't have to talk, because whenever he needed something, he would essentially mime it and someone would get it for him. Speech often inhibits the emotions and obscures the thoughts, while action, or mimed behavior, is living in the most comprehensive sense.

Revealing the psychology of a character's behavior through miming, is the root of all acting. This is how you will duplicate the six personalities of the Creative Wheel of Behavior when creating your Acting for Real characters.

ACTING FOR REAL

The popularity of creating a character for Halloween, charades, and other such parlor games is due to the fact that it allows you to bust out of your comfort zone, see yourself as a different character, and act out a different personality. It allows you to get a glimpse of yourself and release your inhibitions, even for just a moment. Miming characters provides an enjoyable relief from your everyday patterns of behavior.

You must study the positive behaviors and expressive movements of everyday life in order to mime them. Create positive changes in your characters by miming the behaviors of the personalities that you aim to reveal. Model the personalities of people whom you respect and admire. Find role models. Once you understand how to communicate through miming, you will be in control of the mechanics of your characters and have the flexibility of many personalities to portray in your life. A great mime understands that his body is the instrument through which he communicates those mechanics.

Tuning Your Instrument

As an Actor for Real, your body is your most important instrument. It is also the most perfect instrument ever created. Your body is an obedient servant, a receiver and expresser of all human impulses. It is the instrument used to reveal the characters you play. Do not let this perfect and powerful instrument control you. YOU are the director!

In order to direct your instrument, you must be at rest within yourself, in a neutral and balanced posture, in BOP, ready to take action. You need to be in neutral, and from there you can shift into gear. Neutral is a state of rest without bias or prejudice, where you can direct and create conditions. You have the flexibility to observe your body, behavior, and ultimately, your instrument without making judgments.

You shift into a neutral position when you are alone in communion with yourself, stirring in the well of your essence. In neutral, you are simply BEING—the basic experience of being alive and conscious. Meditation and yoga have gained worldwide success because they quiet your mind and bring you back to neutral. When you are in a neutral position you have the option to observe your body and personality. As the director of your life, you can take action now!

Observing Your Body

The human body is capable of hundreds of separate functions: Seeing, hearing, touching, running, dancing, swimming, and digesting to name a few. We are aware of the importance of health and physical fitness. But the almost unlimited potential for enjoyment that the body offers frequently remains unexplored. A bird is born with style. We humans have to create ours. Few learn to move with the grace of an acrobat, see with the fresh eye of an artist, feel the joy of an athlete, or taste with the subtlety of a connoisseur. Because these opportunities are easily within reach, the easiest step toward improving the quality of life consists of simply learning to control the body's senses, emotions, and behaviors.

Everything the body can do is potentially enjoyable. Yet many people ignore this capacity and use their physical equipment as little as possible. We have the most resources to help our citizens stay in shape, yet we are the *least* healthy and fit of *any* nation in the world. Almost 55-percent of American adults are overweight and gaining, while 49-percent of our children are obese. It is obvious that keeping our bodies in shape is not our number one priority, yet it needs to be now more than ever. As an Actor for Real, your desire to be healthy will feed your passion to get fit and tune your instrument. The condition of your instrument determines your quality of life, and your outcomes. It's very simple—if you feel good, you'll be a better Actor for Real!

As every telephone has a specific code number, so every person has a unique behavioral code. When left undeveloped, this code translates chaotic information. An untrained body moves in random and clumsy ways, an insensitive eye presents ugly or uninteresting sights, and the unmusical ear mainly hears jarring noises. If the functions of the body are left to atrophy, the quality of life becomes barely adequate. But if one takes control of what the body can do and learns to impose order on physical sensations, then chaos yields to a sense of enjoyable harmony and consciousness. Use it or lose it!

No matter what you do in life, there is an outcome for it. All behaviors, no matter how strange, have their underlying reasons. Although there is an outcome for everything we do, the fascinating thing about people is that most of the time we do not know the real causes of our outcomes. We think we know, and we are convinced of the motives for our behaviors. But we really can't see ourselves as others see us. That is our challenge.

There is a recorder inside you that has recorded every feeling that your senses have received. You will not be conscious of these feelings and impulses until you learn how to play this recording at will. Feelings cannot be acted unconsciously; they have to be aroused indirectly as emotions. Then you can learn ways to duplicate those emotions as physical behavior. By observing and understanding the way your body functions, mentally and physically, you will be able to use your instrument effectively to accomplish this.

Work in Progress

We hear about people who are "self-made." We're all self-made—it's about working on ourselves one step at a time. You are the only one driving the bus. You are the force behind the creation of your success.

Man is a machine that reacts blindly to external forces. We have no will and very little control of ourselves—that is why we quit so often. Willpower is not psychological; it is mechanical. What we have to study, therefore, is not our psychology, but the mechanics of our instrument. As an Actor for Real, you must understand the importance of working on yourself constantly.

One of my clients, as we were driving along the Pacific Coast Highway, enlightened me with his method of tuning his instrument. "Every day, I would learn something new about myself and my craft that I could apply to my career as a songwriter and musician." The key to his success was working on himself daily, step by step. When you connect one single dot at a time, before you know it, you've drawn a highway.

Real art is knowledge, not talent. To gain anything real, long practice is necessary. Work is transformation. Here's another story to demonstrate the importance of working on oneself.

At one point in the 1960s, I was dropped from my contract at one of the major film studios and was suddenly unemployed. My good friend, restaurateur Red Tracton, got me a bartending job at the Foxhills Country Club. He told me, "If you can learn to make American drinks, you can be an actor anywhere in the world."

I gained a very important life lesson there. I wasn't just a bartender, but a sociologist, therapist, and behavioral expert. Through observing real people, I gathered an arsenal of characters and behaviors to portray as an actor. By working on myself, and increasing my observation of life, I learned how to act.

The lesson is to avoid separating life experiences into, "part of my career," and "not part of my career." Any time that you are working on yourself, you are tuning your instrument and moving towards your goals. YOU are a work in progress. Every waking moment in which you work on yourself contributes to the creation of your enlightenment!

Mine Your Mind

There is gold between them ears pardner! Life is a state of consciousness. But most people walk around in a state of trance. They're just breathing. However, "As a man thinketh in his heart, so is he." You are what you think. Everything you have and do is strictly in accordance with your consciousness. As Barbara Streisand wisely says, "The outside world mirrors what we think of ourselves." You should acknowledge what is right with you every day and the good will grow. Sometimes it is difficult to acknowledge the good when your mind still sees incompleteness and imperfection in many areas of your life. I'm reminded of the often-quoted statement, "What the mind can conceive and believe, the mind can achieve." It sounds like a simple process. It is. But it is not easy.

Maybe you have heard of grabbing the brass ring. The brass ring is within you. In fact, pardner, the brass ring is made of gold! You can grab it and never let go. By constantly working on yourself to be a better, giving, sharing, loving man or woman, you have all the resources already to be that superstar. You are made of the right stuff. You only need to act upon it!

ACTING FOR REAL

Let's Act Now!

As Shakespeare said, we are all actors, so let's act. You are the producer, writer, director and star in your life. You create, direct, and portray many characters every day. The difference is that you deal with real situations and not imaginary ones. Yet by approaching your given circumstances using the same strategies and techniques that an actor uses to develop a character, you are an actor, an Actor for Real.

In order to be a real actor, one must be a real person. A real person can be an actor and a real actor can be a real person. Everyone should be an actor. Everyone can be an actor. Everyone is an actor.

You will now have the ability to act "privately in public" with a sense of logic and truth:

- by understanding how you can develop characters that will empower you.
- by learning how to develop the six components that make up human behavior.

Now you will see which characters you have been revealing and how to stop playing the negative ones. In other words, you can learn how to stop being a bad actor!

This book gives you the tools to develop empowering characters. Using the cliché "from the bedroom to the boardroom," you'll be able to cast yourself as the star in your life. Before you continue, I would like for you to take a minute to prepare yourself for the next act.

Remember a time in your life when learning was fun, exciting, made an impact on you, and changes happened? Now, see yourself there. Got it? Great! Visualize yourself in that picture. What do you see? Do you see yourself in the picture? How do you look? Happy? Excited? Is it in black and white or color? See it in color! What do you hear? People, music, nature? Applause? Praise? What do you feel? What do you smell? What do you taste? Is it sweet? See yourself in that picture. Now project it up onto a drive-in movie screen 60 feet tall. Put a frame of lights around it. Light up the marquee: Starring YOU. Now, hear the sound of 100 soul singers singing, "Go for it!" Make the marquee lights brighter... brighter... Make the singers louder... louder... When it's at its brightest and loudest... make a fist... open your eyes... and shout—"YEAH!"

Now, let's start producing. Let's do it. NOW!

Thom in scenes from the 1971 feature film *Valdez is Coming* starring Burt Lancaster

Burt Lancaster on the cross, Thom pictured behind him
Valdez is Coming

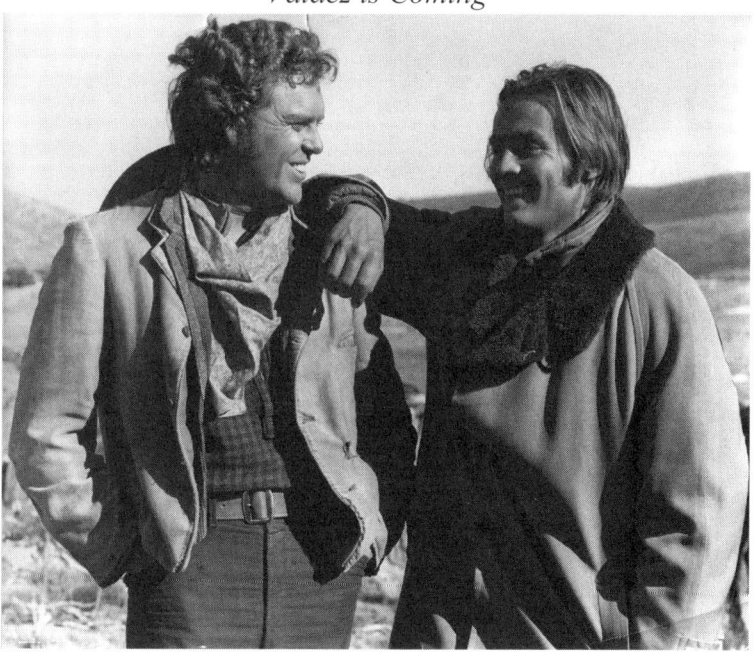

Thom with dear friend, the late Richard Jordan, in scenes
from *Valdez is Coming*

ACTING FOR REAL

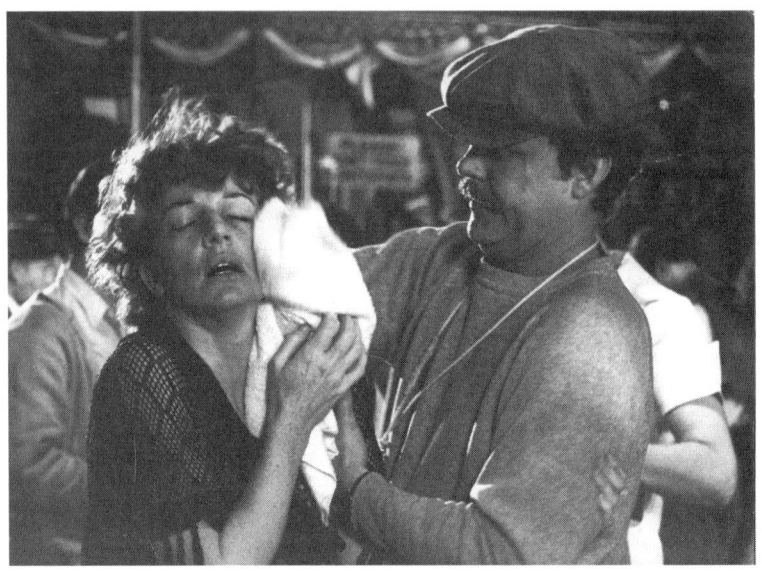

Thom in scenes from the 1969 feature film *They Shoot Horses, Don't They?* with Allyn Ann McLerie

Thom holding Allyn Ann McLerie upside down

Thom in the 1977 classic *Black Sunday* with Marthe
Keller, after filming a scene in which Marthe's
character, Dahlia, shoots him

THE CREATIVE WHEEL
OF EXCELLENCE

CHAPTER 8
YOUR "I AM" PERSONALITY

"I yam what I yam!"
              —Popeye

I AM

Around the turn of the 20th century, Harvard-based philosopher Dr. William James suggested that our personality is a complex structure consisting of an "I" and several "me's." Each of us has a good many roles, or "me's", that we play in various situations. Your roles as son or daughter, student, employee, and so on, all call upon you to modify your behavior at different times, to present yourself differently. Your "I" is your sense of continuous identity, which lies behind these various performances and ties the roles you play together into one "I AM" personality.

If you have ever been forced to perform two different social roles at once (when your parents visit you at college and you must quickly switch personalities from "party animal" to "honor student"), you know how radically different some of our "me's" can be from each other. Our sanity depends, in part, on keeping our various "me's" in their proper place while holding on to a strong sense of our composite "I."

The social psychologist Irving Goffman has analyzed social behavior as if it were a dramatic performance. He finds that most of us have a highly developed ability to play successfully the role demanded from us at each moment. As an Actor for Real, you have rehearsed these roles for years just to portray yourself. You possess a number of different personalities (characters) which you automatically assume for different occasions and with different kinds of people. For example, you play different roles as a daughter, father, son, lover, boyfriend, girlfriend, sister, employee, boss, or friend. Each one is a specific character that you play in life for a specific audience. In your family, you play a certain character. In the workplace, you reveal a different personality. With your friends, you portray a different character. And so on, and so on.

What happens when your repertoire of roles is limited? When you're limited and find yourself without characters to play, or when two different characters clash with each other, you become a bad actor. You lose trust and rapport with others because of your inability to present the personality needed to accomplish your objectives. Unless you have the requisite variety and flexibility to call upon the right character at the right time, you will send mixed messages or no messages at all. You'll be stuck!

When an actor plays a part on the stage or screen, he is given certain objectives for his character to attain in each scene. For instance, he may be required to "get the girl to fall in love with him." If the actor does not have his sexuality personality (one of the six personalities that you are about to learn) rehearsed and at the ready, he will not be able to complete his objective. The same applies to you, the Actor for Real, in each set of circumstances that you are faced with, every day. Having a well rehearsed, diverse set of "I AM" personalities at your fingertips gives you the flexibility you need to obtain the positive outcomes that you desire.

When I am acting, I have to be the conductor in every moment, directing my character's creative triangle (the three behaviors that are his essence—discussed in the proceeding chapters), and taking nothing for granted. It is impossible to leave anything to momentum. I have to direct my character's "I AM" personality and make sure he stays true to his creative triangle. In other words, I have to have a strong sense of my character's "I." A man who has "I" and who knows what is required in every step, can act. A man who has no "I" cannot act. A man's "I" is the heart of each "I AM" personality that he reveals.

"I" = ESSENCE

"AM" = PERSONALITY

Revealing Character Through Behavior

A real actor is one who creates and who reveals, not conceals, his emotions. All roles are built out of such straightforward behavior. Only in his own and other people's imaginations does the actor appear to create. In actual fact, he cannot create. He only can duplicate the personality of the "I AM" character, through behavior. An actor cannot know what emotions or thoughts another person possesses. He cannot feel what another person feels. But if he plays a part, he must have enough understanding and feelings for the part in order to duplicate them through his actions.

And this is so with every profession in which special knowledge is required. The artist without knowledge only imagines. Only if we know the psychology of the character's "I AM" personality can we understand how to reveal it. If we do not know what our objective is, or how to recreate the right character to attain it, our roles are limited. If this is the perpetual story of your life, then you exist on autopilot—acting out of sheer habit rather than by decisively performing the specific actions and behaviors needed to attain your objectives. By making the effort to turn off this autopilot, you will break the cycle of habit and bring yourself into present time where positive change will happen. You'll BUST out of that comfort zone!

We are about to start the work that I call—THE PROCESS. The objective of this is to understand what is happening around you, and to develop a personally meaningful sense of what your life experience is all about. From that will come the profound joy of "I AM who I AM." The most important thing you will ever learn is the "I AM" process.

The Creative Wheel of Behavior that I am about to introduce to you, is the process for discovering your composite "I AM." The Creative Wheel is the six components that make up human behavior (humanities, sexuality, humor, power, danger, and vulnerability), all externally based, that you will learn to reveal through individual "I AM" personalities.

CHAPTER 9
THE CREATIVE WHEEL OF BEHAVIOR

"Sow a thought and reap an act. Sow an act, and you reap a habit. Sow a habit, and you reap a character. Sow a character, and you reap a destiny."
—Charles Reade

"Be more concerned with your character than your reputation."
—John Wooden

The Creative Wheel of Behavior contains the six externally based components that make up human behavior, divided into two creative triads or triangles: the enlightened and the dark. In this section, you will discover and learn to reveal the behaviors in each triad using active reasoning. The Creative Wheel gives you the flexibility and options needed to reach your objectives, by giving you various characters ("I AM" personalities) to portray in life. The characters are based on the triads, and their comprised creative triangles, with minor adaptations made to meet each of your outcomes. The Creative Wheel is the foundation for all of your Acting for Real characters!

CREATIVE WHEEL DEPICTION EXERCISE

Get out your journal and answer these questions, observing the following diagram of the Creative Wheel of Behavior. Which behaviors of the wheel do you think describe you? Which describe other people you know? Do the words in the wheel evoke any particular emotions or meanings at first glance?

ACTING FOR REAL

You must identify any negative or counterproductive beliefs that you have regarding these six behaviors, before you can use them effectively to create your new, empowered life characters. Remember, garbage in = garbage out.

The Creative Wheel of Human Behavior

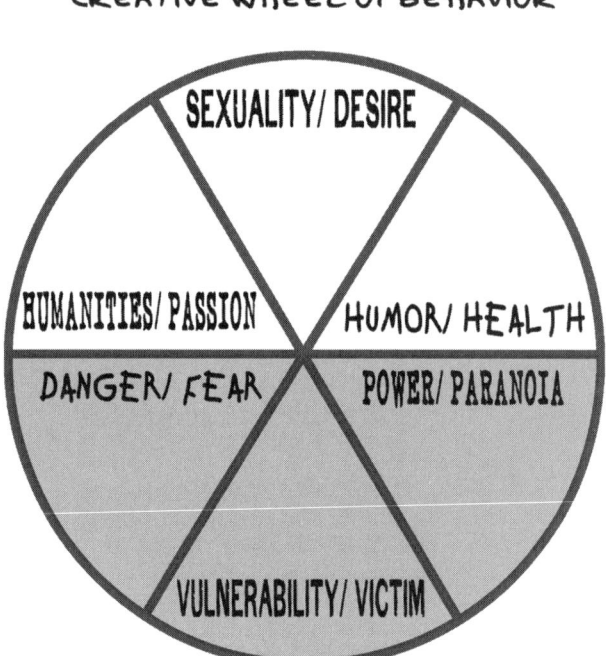

CREATIVE WHEEL OF BEHAVIOR

The Creative Triangles

The creative triangle is about change. Flux is the very essence of life. Observe that each of the triads that make up the Creative Wheel of Excellence (the enlightened and the dark) contains three sections. The use of the number three is intentional.

Aristotle declared that all things are three and that three is everywhere. First there is action, our desire to change an active force within us. Second, there is passivity, the resistance of old habits (inertia of the familiar) and our innate dislike of effort and change.

Without a third force, these two opposing forces counterbalance each other, or revolve around each other so that nothing happens. The solution becomes the problem and the problem is the solution. For example, you can't bake bread without three ingredients: water, flour, and fire.

When a third, or activating force, appears in the form of new knowledge, or in the learning of a special technique for bringing about change, action happens. We begin to use our minds quite differently. As Einstein said, "We can't solve problems by using the same kind of thinking we used when we created them." With the help of a third, conducting force, something new begins to happen!

An actor becomes an actor either because he needs to exploit his own personality, or the very opposite. He may, and many actors do, have a need to become a lot of other people. You, as an Actor for Real in your own life, are no different. You have certain predominant traits that should be understood and nurtured. These are the traits that make up your creative triangle. Trying to create traits that are not included in your triangle is a waste of your time, just as neglecting to portray traits that are included in your triangle is counterproductive. This is why great casting is a much celebrated and most sought-after skill in making movies. Do you know how to cast yourself in your own life? Are you the class clown? The victim? The angry beast? The sex kitten? The humanitarian? The greedy monster?

Over the years as an observer, teacher, and coach I have found that most people in our society, unfortunately, play the vulnerability character of the wheel—the victim. "Woe is me!", "Why me?" Resigning yourself to play the victim in life is a matter of attitude. The fact is that it's easier to give up and be the victim ("it's not my fault I'm not successful") than it is to make a concerted effort to succeed. As you've learned, the road to success requires extensive self-exploration and a heightened level of awareness, which is sometimes painful. The victim character would rather sit back, believe his inner critic that he can't do it, and give up all hope of reaching his goals and positive outcomes.

In addition to this, the victim character is driven by negative belief systems that are fed constantly by societal myths and clichés. We're barraged constantly by millions of reasons not to try, based on education, odds of success, ethnicity, and belief in a doomed fate ("What can you do?" and "These are the cards I've been dealt, I have to play them."). We are constantly receiving garbage, which is no more than the byproducts of other people's belief systems. If we take in the garbage, that is exactly what we put out. Hence, the victim character that most of society has resigned to playing.

The enlightened triangle of the Creative Wheel will give you characters to play that will overpower the victim character by cutting off its supply of negative beliefs, and replacing them with positive, empowering beliefs. Once it has run out of excuses, the victim character will destroy itself and you will be on a clear path towards your goals!

Revealing your "I AM" Personalities

Silent emotional expression (mime) is familiar to almost everyone in the world. It is a universal form of self-expression built upon instinct and basic human communication skills. That is why it will be easy for you to learn to reveal the "I AM" personalities that make up your new empowered life character. You already know how to imitate by instinct and observation. Monkey see, monkey do! We're just going to fine tune the instrument that is already there.

To reveal your "I AM" personalities, you must first learn to externally duplicate the specific behaviors of each of the characters you wish to portray. Those external behaviors will then be plugged into the corresponding internal emotions that drive each "I AM" personality. The result is that each of your "I AM" personalities will be revealed by a magnetic force, bringing your new empowered characters to life!

While all behavior is externally based, if the external is not connected to the internal, it has no substance, nor will the characters you portray. You will be nothing more than an automaton, a machine moving blindly in a mechanical way. The external needs to be connected to the internal in order to connect you with your emotions, your magnet. When you are revealing any of your enlightened personalities, this is your outcome—magnetic presence.

Psychological gesture is the process used to connect your external behaviors and internal emotions to create magnetic presence. For you, as the Actor for Real, this is the next step in the process of understanding how to develop and reveal your "I AM" personalities.

The psychological gesture, first identified by the great Russian director and teacher Michael Chekhov, is the key to revealing the actor's subconscious. It is a focused and repeatable movement or action that awakens the actor's emotional life, and its kinesthetic image feeds him while he acts on stage. Every character, according to Chekhov, possesses a single psychological gesture which reveals his secret, innermost motivation and personality trait. You will discover at least one duplicable psychological gesture to reveal each of your enlightened personalities.

The movement that forms the basis of the psychological gesture may be as abstract and fantastic as an arm stretching endlessly through an imaginary prison window (Chekhov's psychological gesture for Hamlet). Or as concrete and realistic as the stroking of a cat while softly speaking of the heartless destruction of Russia's gentry, a gesture traditionally associated with Lenin. "Through the psychological gesture," Chekhov wrote, "the soul of the character and the physical body of the performer meet."

By being observant and then taking action, you can reveal your enlightened personalities through the use of psychological gesture. To learn how to duplicate the enlightened "I AM" personalities, you must remove yourself from the given circumstances of your life and observe other people and what they do to reveal the humanities, humor, and sexuality in their behavior. Practice modeling the best examples. Model the best to be the best!

The first three "I AM" personalities that we will explore are the enlightened behaviors that will form your new life character: Humanities/ Passion, Sexuality/ Desire, and Humor/ Health. You will observe how these behaviors complement one another and work together to create the empowered character that will drive you to success.

The Creative Wheel

Now, using the wheel and its triangles, let's discover how to develop Acting for Real characters that will empower you, rekindle your humanity and passion for life, find your sense of humor, and reveal your sexuality. We'll also learn how to avoid the abyss of the dark triangle: the Power, Danger, and Vulnerability personalities. Using the Creative Wheel, you'll discover how to bust out of your comfort zone, nuke the victim character, create empowered Acting for Real characters that will strengthen your self-esteem, and change your personal life's history so it maximally supports your life's outcomes.

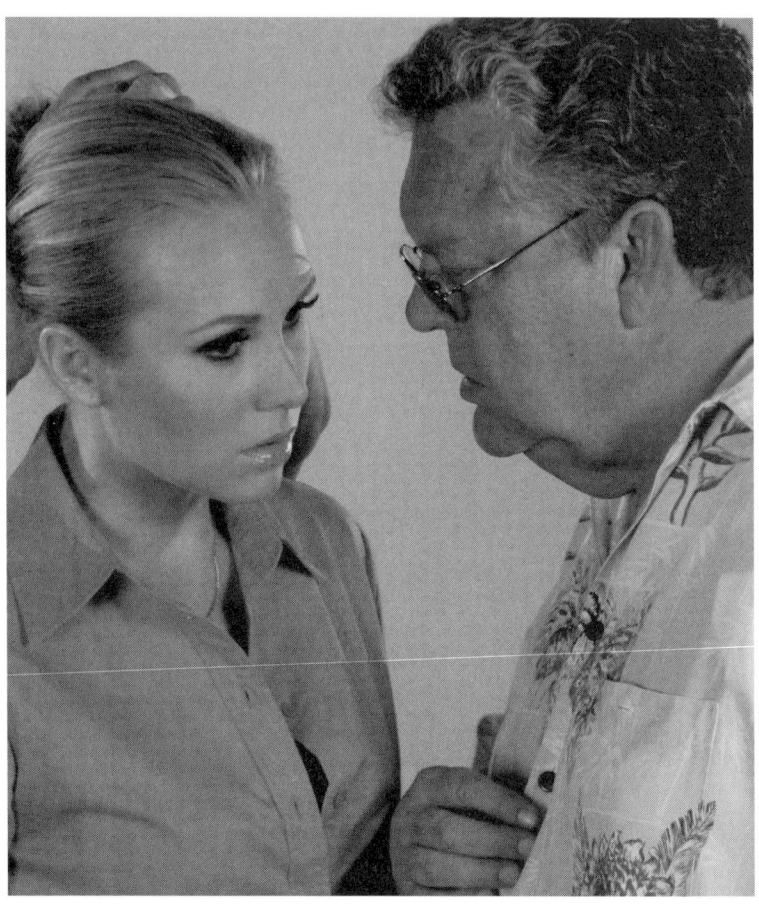

Actress Alana Curry and Thom working on the set of
GoPotato.tv's *Sweet Dreams* series

CHAPTER 10
THE ENLIGHTENED TRIANGLE

"In this world, which is so plainly the antechamber of another, there are no happy men. The true division of humanity is between those who live in light and those who live in darkness. Our aim must be to diminish the number of the latter and increase the number of the former."
—*Victor Hugo*

A great attitude, positive belief system, duplicating behavior, understanding your "I AM," and being in BOP, make up the foundation upon which the enlightened triangle functions. The character that you portray in life is based on your creative triangle, 50% is one behavior of the Creative Wheel, with two supporting behaviors representing the two 25% pieces.

You will now learn to mold your triangle, and thus your "I," to reflect the three enlightened behaviors (Humanities, Humor, and Sexuality) that will drive you to success. The characters of the enlightened triangle will give you the control over the tools that you need to reach your positive outcomes. As an Actor for Real, the enlightened triangle is the formula for your new empowered life characters.

The enlightened triangle is composed of the three "I AM" personalities that will break the cycle of mechanical habit—your autopilot. This triad of externally based behaviors will allow you to release your body from its conditioned constraints and free you to go after your positive outcomes with passion, humor, and heat.

ACTING FOR REAL

Let's break the chains of habit and use the enlightened "I AM" personalities to empower you!

The Enlightened Triangle

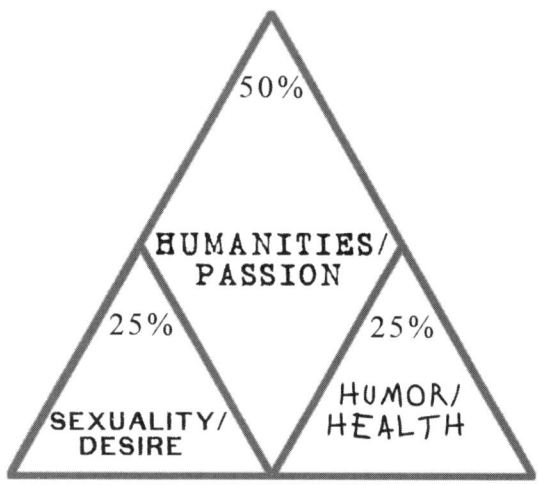

CASE STUDY

One of my students is a young lady from a small Western town who exudes passionate energy and humor in every moment. She is very sexual, in the sense that she is uninhibited and unembarrassed by her body in the healthiest of ways.

What's her triangle?
50%—Sexuality
25%—Humor
25%—Humanities

Now that she understands her triangle, she can nurture and role-play each part of it. She can become such an expert on "herself" that when auditioning for characters with similar triangles, there will be few better actresses for the part than her.

On the flip side, the actress can use the remaining sections of the wheel (Danger, Power, and Vulnerability) as the "dark side" of characters she plays to give them depth, while still expertly "leading" with the predominant traits (Sexuality, Humor, Humanities).

Now all of her characters and roles, in acting and in life, will have specificity, depth, and be as real as she is. By understanding and taking ownership of your enlightened triangle, and duplicating these behaviors with specificity, you will significantly increase your chances of attaining your objectives. In other words, you will finally be driving the bus!

HUMANITIES

Thom as Hugh Cleveland in the 1983 miniseries
The Winds of War

CHAPTER 11
HUMANITIES
PASSION

"We must act out passion before we can feel it."
— *Jean-Paul Sartre*

"Passion is in all great searches and is necessary to all creative endeavors."
— *Eugene W. Smith*

"I AM" Humanities/ Passion

hu·man·i·ties (n. pl.)
1. The qualities of being humane; benevolent.
2. Humane characteristics, attributes, or acts.

pas·sion (n.)
1. Boundless enthusiasm.

Man's desires and strivings in life are first prompted by his feelings, emotions, and beliefs. He has always responded more quickly whenever his emotions, and therefore his imagination, have been aroused to the level of passion. His imagination has not only been the starting point, but the driving force that produces his outcomes. All religions, adventures, systems of education, discoveries in art and science, and all forms of sport and business, are expressed through some force of emotional action; in other words, through the medium of behavior. "Humanities/ Passion" is the first example of that behavior.

The first enlightened "I AM" personality is Humanities/ Passion. It is the most powerful "I AM" because it reveals passionate and total commitment to your self-worth. Your "I AM" Humanities/ Passion personality represents the power of your belief system and what you stand for.

While we were appalled by the horrific terrorist actions of 9-11-01, these events were a major shift in the emotional paradigm of the human race. People reached out to contribute financial aid, emotional support, and loving, altruistic thoughts. These are perfect examples of revealing humanities on a massive scale. But the terrorists had similar feelings of passion. As crazy as it may seem to us, they also thought that they were revealing their humanities. They were mining a belief system in which they were passionately committed. Even when revealing humanities, there are many sides. We in our society have trouble understanding the use of suicide missions to make a statement. But whether your belief system is right or wrong in the eyes of society, if you believe in it passionately, it will reveal itself with emotional energy and power. This is your chance to discover which core beliefs truly make you passionate, and to make sure that they are rooted in a motivation to help mankind.

Every professional who provides a service to mankind, including doctors, lawyers, teachers, police officers, politicians, religious leaders, and firefighters, is a humanitarian at heart. Even if they seem to lose their passion for their work over a period of time and become jaded, they will reveal their humanities in some way or another. This "I AM" personality is the foundation of their belief system—it has to be. Humanities and passion are the essence of who they are and what they do.

Duplicating the "I AM" Humanities Personality

As you learned in BOP, observation is the key to self-awareness and change. So do you see yourself as a humanitarian? If you do, how does it manifest itself in your behavior? Do you get excited about your political convictions and passionately jump onto your soapbox on election day? How far do you go with your emotions and energy to prove a point or that you're right? Do you have any of these qualities? Does any of this sound familiar to you? If you answered, "YES!" to any of these, at some time or another you have revealed to your audience your "I AM" Humanities/ Passion personality.

Make a list of everything that you are "for" in life. What are you willing to debate or argue about? What is important to you? What do you stand for? Who are you? What are your causes?

For example, here's mine:

1) Education —I'm pro-education and passionately in favor of a superior reading level across the board!
2) Enlightenment —People should be working on themselves throughout their lives; Rekindle the higher power within you!
3) Environmentalism —Save the earth! Stop polluting! Recycle! Hybrid vehicles for everyone!
4) Pro-Arts and Humanities —Stop cutting the arts and humanities education in our public schools!

Get out your journal and make your list. Now, stand up and read it out loud. Observe what your voice does as your level of passion fluctuates.

I would encourage everyone to take voice lessons to bring even further control to the enlightened characters that you are learning to reveal. Not only is it great therapy, it is also a confidence builder. I can hear some of you saying, "But I don't have the money to take a voice lesson!" or "I can't sing!"—Snap out of it! Stop playing the victim character! Join the church choir and ask the choir leader to give you voice lessons. The choir leader is a humanitarian and would love to help!

For you to be able to reveal your "I AM" Humanities/ Passion personality, you have to get involved in life! Be a volunteer! Give back!

Here is an exercise to give you more fun ways to duplicate and reveal your "I AM" Humanities/ Passion personality.

AWARDS NIGHT EXERCISE

Observe the behavior of the award recipient. These are humanitarian speeches coming from love and a cause. The acceptance speech is where the recipients connect their external behavior with their internal emotions and passion.

Internal —their cause and love of mankind, and devotion to those who helped drive them to success.

External —revealing that passion through psychological gesture.

Practice giving your own award acceptance speech, duplicating some of the psychological gestures you observed on award shows.

Examples of humanities performances by actors to model:

Russell Crowe —*Gladiator*
Robin Wright —*Forrest Gump*
Tom Hanks —*Philadelphia*
Julia Roberts —*Erin Brokovich*
Robert Redford —*All The President's Men*
Marlon Brando —*On The Waterfront*
Meryl Streep —*Sophie's Choice*

Here are some more role models for you. Observe television evangelists and preachers. What do you see? What kind of psychological gestures do they make? The movements of their arms are generally uplifting and energetic as they move about, almost in a dance. They are charged with magnetic presence with which they attract their audience.

Next, watch some politicians and activists. What do they have in common? Their physical gestures include clenched fists, sawing the air, hands over their heads, strong emotions in their voices —their entire bodies vibrate with power and forcefulness.

Have you ever gotten up in the morning on the wrong side of the bed? Ever have a case of the "Monday morning blues"? Now, hold your hands above your head, palms up and facing out, reaching toward the sky. Hold this pose for one minute. You cannot do that and stay depressed! It's physically impossible. While doing this exercise, let every emotion that is pulling you down fly out through your fingertips.

ACTING FOR REAL

Go back to your "soapbox list" again. Get up on a chair, the couch, or anything that will make you taller. Climb a mountain! Get that feeling that you are above everyone else. Use the psychological gesture that you just learned (palms out, arms outstretched overhead). Now you're ready to do some preachin' about your causes!

Let the emotions wash over you! Don't censor yourself! Have fun! You're connecting with yourself while conveying your passion to others! Do these exercises every day for a few minutes, using each of your impassioned causes. Try them in different movements and positions—standing, sitting, walking, moving, etc. The most important thing is to keep your psychological gesture above your heart at all times. You can't get excited about anything with your arms hanging lifelessly at your sides, just as you can't be depressed about anything with your hands up over your head! Keep your dukes up!

After doing this for a period of time by yourself, try it out in front of other people. Observe yourself when you're talking to someone about one of your causes, take note of the psychological gestures that excite them, and remember to duplicate those gestures next time. Congratulations, you have now successfully revealed and taken ownership of your "I AM" Humanities/ Passion personality!

Now go out and find your passion!

SEXUALITY

Sally Kellerman and Thom on the set of the 1985 feature
film *Moving Violations*

CHAPTER 12
SEXUALITY
DESIRE

"Sexuality is the lyricism of the masses."
              —Charles Baudelaire

ACTING FOR REAL

The next enlightened "I AM" personality of your empowered life character is "Sexuality/ Desire." Your "I AM" Sexuality/ Desire personality gives you the ability to reveal mental and physical desire. Before we get started in learning how to duplicate the behaviors of, and reveal this often misunderstood personality, let's take a moment to explore sexuality.

sex·u·al·i·ty (n.)
1. The condition of being characterized and distinguished by sex.

Sex

During recent years, millions of people, men and women alike, around the world have tuned in to watch the sexy antics of Carrie, Samantha, Miranda, & Charlotte on HBO's hit series, *Sex and the City*. I have to admit that while I am not a huge television aficionado, those sexy girls have reeled me in. Sunday nights just wouldn't be the same for me without watching their adventures of love, desire, relationships, and more importantly, what draws most people...SEX. That show has turned the act of revealing sexuality into an art form!

Sex sells. The most highly rated shows on television are makeover shows. The first step in making you over is revealing your sexuality! So those shows hire the best makeup and hair people, get the best clothes, and bring people out to their spouses and say,"WOW! Doesn't he/ she look hot!"

The problem is that the hair goes limp, the makeup starts to run, and the clothes go back to the cleaners. That feeling is instant gratification, a momentary feeling that is seldom reproduced. This reminds me of the Chinese Proverb, "If you give a man a fish, you have fed him for a day. If you teach a man to fish, you have fed him for a lifetime." I'm going to teach you how to duplicate that sexy feeling and KEEP IT! So you can reveal your sexuality—any time, any place.

Sexuality

Why does sex frequently scare the living daylights out of us? Let's talk about how healthy and important sex is to your happiness, health, and success!

A list of truths:

Sexuality doesn't mean sex.
Sexuality is healthy.
Sexuality is a motivator.
Sexuality builds self-esteem.

Sexuality is a useful tool to better yourself. Sexual attraction is normal human behavior. Every person is able to respond to sexual stimulation. While this response is never exactly the same in any two individuals, its basic physiological pattern is similar in all men and women. Men and women can be sexually aroused at nearly all times, in many different ways, and by a great variety of stimuli.

ACTING FOR REAL

Sexual behavior produces many changes in the human body, such as an increase in pulse rate and blood pressure, muscular contractions, and many other signs of mounting excitement and arousal.

The human body is very complex. All responses and actions produce and need certain chemicals to complete themselves. The chemical epinephrine is produced by sexual arousal. Epinephrine is a chemical naturally and sometimes artificially produced, that speeds up all bodily processes and functions. It's good for you!

Sexuality is a part of nature—the courting, the attraction, the dance, etc., are natural instincts that we suppress because we are afraid of the fear generated by society, that if we reveal our sexuality we are morally weak (GI=GO). But that's not at all true! Sex is healthy. Sex is a dance. Sexuality releases hormones and enzymes when you are magnetically attracted to someone.

When you see someone you are attracted to, what happens? When you fantasize about someone, what happens to you? How do you reveal the desire that you are feeling inside? Once you can learn to reveal your sexuality, using it as a tool to build self-confidence and win your goals, you can use it as the fire that fuels your enlightened triangle!

Desire

"Those who restrain desire, do so because theirs is weak enough to be restrained."
                    —William Blake

"Her kisses left something to be desired—the rest of her."
—*Anonymous*

de·sire (v.)
1. The natural longing that is excited by the enjoyment or the thought of any good, and impels to action or effort its continuance or possession;
2. An eager wish to obtain or enjoy; an object of longing; lust; appetite.

Desire begins in the mind—and I don't mean sex fantasies. Intellect is stimulating, and, as you will find out in the next chapter, humor is sexy. So while physical attraction is necessary, mental attraction is by far the more powerful of the two types of attraction (mental desire can become physical desire, but physical desire does not necessarily lead to mental desire).

But there is a difference between physical desire (lust) and mental desire (love). Sexual desire is a powerful physical excitement. Love is a powerful caring for someone else. It can also be physically exciting. Love can exist without sexual desire, and sexual desire can exist without love. Many people are happiest when both partners share both love and sexual desire. Therefore, as you learn to reveal your "I AM" Sexuality/ Desire personality, you will begin to discover qualities that reveal the mental and physical desire that draws you to someone, and vice versa.

ACTING FOR REAL

Revealing Sexuality

Being successful at revealing sexuality is a decision, a choice—regardless of your age, size, ethnic background, educational background, or current economic situation. Regardless of media trends (trend is the key word here) there is no absolute standard for what is sexy. Who each of us finds sexy is a matter of personal taste. While there are some people a lot of us find quite sexy, no one person is going to be sexy to everyone, even Pamela Anderson, Cindy Crawford, Tom Cruise, or Leonardo DiCaprio.

One of the things I learned a long time ago about success in general is that successful people aren't the most beautiful, the most talented, or the most intelligent. Successful people (in any area of life) are simply the ones who decide that they deserve to win, and don't stop until they've achieved their goals. And the same applies to revealing your sexuality.

Have you ever wondered how movie stars keep reinventing themselves? Have you noticed that many stars are not physically attractive, but you find them attractive anyway? How do they do it? They do it by developing various "I AM" Sexuality/ Desire personalities that they call upon to portray.

When actors reveal sexuality, they bring heat to the part and stimulate our own sexual desires and fantasies, etc. You can too! Have some fun, play dress up, and reveal your "I AM" Sexuality/ Desire personality using these excellent role models.

Kim Cattrall —*Sex in the City*
Gwyneth Paltrow —*Great Expectations*
Britney Spears —"MTV Music Video Awards"
Leonardo DiCaprio —*Titanic*
Brad Pitt —*Thelma & Louise*
Sharon Stone —*Basic Instinct*
Richard Gere —*An Officer and a Gentleman*
Madonna —*Truth or Dare*
Raquel Welch —*One Million Years B.C.*
Marilyn Monroe —*The Seven-Year Itch*
Mel Gibson —*Lethal Weapon*

What is the psychological gesture that all of these star performances have in common that you can model? They are all, in one way or another, flirting with YOU the audience!

How do you reveal sexuality so it becomes a permanent part of your character? How do you cast yourself in those parts? First, you need to learn to be comfortable with less physical space. Think of it as a dance. The Europeans are masters at this dance. They lean forward when someone is talking to them, but not close enough to do a dental examination. They touch you, something awkward to most Americans. They are not afraid to express affection. Lord knows the first 20 minutes of any French dinner party is spent distributing the kisses. It is an excellent tradition by the way. And let's not be mistaken; they REALLY do kiss you on the cheeks, unlike the Hollywood air kisses method.

Revealing sexuality is a 25-degree shift in your physical behavior and body language. This creates an angle, so your body is not aligned as a perfectly even square. Nobody's going to flirt with a square! Revealing sexuality is a drop of your shoulder, tilt of your head, a coy glance, a pouty mouth, licking your lips, tossing your hair, or crossing your legs. Recognize any of these? Whichever ones you don't already do—add to your arsenal of duplicable behaviors. Use these to reveal your "I AM" Sexuality/ Desire personality!

Flirting

flirt (v.)
   1.   To make playfully romantic or sexual overtures.

"Did the sun come out, or did you just smile at me?"

"If I told you that you had a great body, would you hold it against me?"

"You're so beautiful that you made me forget my pickup line!"

In a recent study, 46% of the men surveyed said women would be flattered by flirting, while only 5% of the women agreed. Clearly, behavior that some people see as harmless fun, or even flattery, may be considered harassment by others.

Sounds pretty serious! When did flirting, one of the first steps in the mating dance, not to mention such a fun and potent way of revealing the "I AM" Sexuality/ Desire personality, become such a source of anxiety? Even back in Victorian novels, it seems that flirting was a normal practice. And they were supposed to be the uptight generation! What's got our panties in a bunch?

The human race was made to interact with both sexes, and one major way of meeting new people involves the act of flirting. Flirting is not only a good way to meet other people, but it's also a great way to build a relationship with someone, and in the process build self-confidence for YOU!

Self-confidence comes from self-esteem. Self-esteem is liking and accepting yourself. It is being comfortable with yourself. It is feeling that you deserve to be treated well and deserve to be respected. Therefore, when you flirt, it doesn't mean that you're weak morally. It's fuel for your self-confidence.

I have always admired people who could flirt well. It's a way to reveal your natural, healthy feelings without suppressing them. Plus, it's a great ego boost when you know someone is flirting with you. Even if it's when you're stopped at a red light and the person in the next car is checking you out. Resist the impulse to hide, and instead use it as a safe opportunity to practice your flirting skills!

Pageant contestants have coaches who have helped them hone the act of flirting down to a science, finding just the right combination of self-confidence and sincerity. "I want you to like me because I like you" is what makes the difference between getting the tiara and getting zip.

Like mime, flirting comes naturally to everybody. We've all seen how babies do it. But for a lot of us, it's an instinct that we neglect as we grow up. As we lose our self-confidence, flirting becomes frightening. In reality, it's something you should enjoy because it puts you in the driver's seat. Flirting reveals that you are not afraid to share you, at that moment, with somebody else. Whenever you flirt with someone, you are sharing that moment in time.

Let's face it—we could all use a refresher course on how to reveal sexuality through flirting! I observed one of my acting students in particular. Her flirting abilities were an art form. She was amazing—old men, young women, no one got by without getting flirted with. She radiates heat and is not afraid to show it!

Heat

heat (n.)
1. Intensity, as of passion, emotion, color, appearance, or effect.
2. To excite the feelings of; inflame.
3. To become excited emotionally or intellectually.

Each one of us, in our unique way, has been filled with heat and fire. As children, we are walking little bundles of fire! Remember a time, as a child, when you were full of fiery passion and heat over something you desired to accomplish? Have you ever wished you could recreate that awesome feeling?

How do you radiate your heat? One of my teachers, George Shdanoff, who was a protégé of Michael Chekhov, taught me a method of sustaining, holding, and revealing radiation—i.e. HEAT!

First use your imagination, the "magic if." Suppose that there's a fire in front of you (a campfire, fireplace, etc.). Feel the heat against your body, like the sun beating down on you while you're sunbathing. Now take that feeling of heat and connect it with your internal light, the fire that drives you. Take your hand in a gesture, and practice radiating that light through your fingers. Remember this is not a nuclear experiment—lighten up. It's a game! The light is within you. You have the source.

Now have some fun! Practice sending your heat to other people. As you extend your hand, imagine that you are projecting that heat over a distance to the person next to you whom you're talking to or the person you're flirting with across the room. If you successfully connect your external heat with your internal light source, you will be instantly connected with the other person.

This is called putting your attention on your subject. If you do that while you're listening, talking, or simply being present, you will be generating, projecting, and ultimately extending your light to others. If you are flirting, you need to make sure that you're sending your attention to the other person. Without your attention, you won't be able to send your light, or your heat.

If your attention is not there, your heat will be dispersed into the atmosphere, never reaching the other person at all! What you need to do is listen while you're sending your light to the other person. Watch while you're sending your light. Observe the fulfillment of the gesture that you have just initiated. Allow the other person the completion and fulfillment of the gesture, by putting your full attention on their response.

STOKE YOUR FIRE EXERCISE

Imagine that you're in front of that bonfire again. It's hot enough to scorch a marshmallow! Move as close as possible towards it. Feel the heat on your face, your hands, and the rest of your body. Look at the power the fire has, the color of the flames that shoot up in the air. Experience this feeling and move with it, by speaking, handling objects, and believing in your imagination. The heat of the fire comes from your belly, which is the furnace of your emotions. Ever hear the phrase, "He has no fire in his belly" or on the flip side, "When she walked in, she lit up the room!"

Once you've imagined this, let it penetrate you. Feel your body filled with heat and power. Radiate the light from your forehead, chest, hands, and fingertips, and extend the fire beyond your circle of attention (into the next room or right in front of you). Imagine yourself writing your name in the air with the light, to get the feeling of extending your energy further than you ever have. Feel the fire permeating your body and lighting up the darkness that used to surround you. By doing this, you are radiating heat and power. This is what makes the enlightened triangle the light triangle—in the truest sense of the word!

Fire is the quality that you must have to ignite your enlightened triangle!

HUMOR

Thom featured as "Mr. P", the Elvis School of Impersonators
Instructor, in the 1983 hit series *Sledge Hammer*

CHAPTER 13
HUMOR
HEALTH

"WARNING: Humor may be hazardous to your illness."
                    —Ellie Katz

The "I AM" Personality that completes your enlightened triangle,
is "Humor/ Health." If you've ever had a good belly laugh and felt
GREAT afterwards, then you understand how the two go hand in

hand. Your "I AM" Humor/ Health personality allows you to reveal your enlightened triangle with lightness and case.

hu·mor (n.)
1. The quality that makes something laughable or amusing; funniness.
2. That which is intended to induce laughter or amusement.
3. The ability to perceive, enjoy, or express what is amusing, comical, incongruous, or absurd.

health (n.)
1. The overall condition of an organism at a given time.
2. Soundness, especially of body or mind; freedom from disease or abnormality;
3. A condition of optimal well-being.

Are you afraid to be funny? Why should you be funny? Keep in mind that what is funny for one person is not necessarily funny to another. Depending on such things as health, culture, and background, people may have varied responses to and perspectives on different types of humor. But one thing is for sure, as *Reader's Digest* has said for years, "laughter is the best medicine." Even when you roll back time, and recall a particularly difficult experience in your life, you'll usually relate that experience with humor. Your nervous system won't let you re-create the same kind of pain that you felt before. Those who laugh, live longer. Humor is health—physically, mentally, and emotionally. Humor protects as it empowers. Therefore, by revealing the "I AM" Humor/ Health personality in balance with the Humanities and Sexuality personalities that you have just learned, you are portraying an enlightened, empowered character to the world.

Benefits of Humor

You may have noticed that when you are having fun and laughing, you feel better than when you are sad and brooding! A sense of humor and two of its counterparts can contribute to your personal health. The first beneficial humorous trait is being able to laugh at yourself, and the second is the act of laughter itself. Laughter causes the full action of the diaphragm, thus benefiting the whole cardiovascular system, because of the amount of oxygen taken in during laughter. During laughter, the whole body is revitalized by an internal massage!

Laughter also increases your metabolism, your muscles are stimulated and neurochemicals called catecholamines enter your bloodstream, improving the efficiency of all of your bodily functions.

A specific example of laughter during serious illness is included in Norman Cousin's book, *Anatomy of an Illness*. Former editor of *The Saturday Review*, Cousins had a very serious and painful disorder of the connective tissue collagen (his cells were literally coming apart). The pain medications doctors gave him were seldom effective and he was often in excruciating pain. Doctors set his recovery chances at one in 500.

ACTING FOR REAL

Cousins decided that humor might be an answer. He arranged for videotapes of old *Candid Camera* shows and other old comedy shows to be shown at his hospital bedside. After a few hours of genuine belly-laughing fun, Cousins was entirely pain-free for hours more, and sometimes even days. And despite the odds, he ultimately recovered.

Studies also show that laughter can help defeat infection by assisting the immune system. According to one study, laughter increases an antibody in the saliva that lowers a person's susceptibility to upper respiratory illness. The levels of this antibody were higher in those who regularly use humor to face life's problems. Cortisol, an immune suppresser, has a tremendous influence on the system. Laughter decreases cortisol, which allows interleuken-2 and other immune boosters to express themselves.

Like all of the behaviors of the enlightened triangle, humor and health are interdependent. When you feel good, things seem more humorous, and when you laugh you feel better. "OK!", you say, "Sounds good, but how do I get to be funny?"

Being Funny

Do you consider yourself a funny person? Being funny is the most important and FUN way of revealing your "I AM" Humor personality. Humor equals surprise. If you can surprise someone, or catch them off guard using humor as your weapon of choice, you can be funny. If you can surprise yourself, that's even better.

Think funny! Humor is easier to recognize than to analyze. Look at the world around you. You don't have to study life under a microscope, but observe something or someone closely enough and you'll soon find something humorous about it—guaranteed! Realize also that it does not have to be accepted by everyone to be considered funny.

The ability to be funny depends on a person's ability to trust the right side of their brain to be creative. Have fun and let it roll. If you question your own humor, the left brain will kick in and reject your humorous thoughts. Remember that your left brain is the logical, critical side of your brain—where your inner critic resides. If you listen to your inner critic, you will never be funny. When the left brain hears a statement that is not logical, the creative right side of the brain will adapt its own meaning, with the resulting "funny" feeling that goes with it. Thus, we have the resulting laughter.

Adapt material! Humor can be from any source, from anyone, and from anywhere. It's a universal language, which can be adapted to any situation. When adapting humor, degenderize it, de-race it, and apply it to your life. Look around you. The world is crazy if you see it that way. So think crazy and you will be crazy. Funny how that is!

Don't be afraid to laugh at yourself. People are more apt to accept someone open, vulnerable, and trusting. When you are able to laugh at yourself, people are more willing to accept kidding and jokes about themselves from you too.

ACTING FOR REAL

Share your humor! Tell your latest joke. Share a funny story. I always make my students learn to tell at least two jokes—yet another tool in the arsenal of your "I AM" Humor personality. In this way, you can provide laughter and happiness to others, giving someone else a new perspective on life. You can take almost any negative situation, injustice or difficult situation, and use humor to turn things around for the better. When combined with passion and heat, humor is the tool of empowerment!

Humor can create an atmosphere where difficult situations are defused and turned around for a positive outcome. Even the sourest grouch will smile a little inside, when their funny bone is stroked. Choose the type of humor that stretches your comfort zone. Don't use humor that can be used against you at some future date. Off color humor can and will be used against you. To protect yourself, be tasteful. Swearing is just a lazy way to shock the mind. The name of the humor game is: keep it clean, talk about situations, yourself, and stay away from stereotyping people into groups. Then deliver your humor with passion, animation, and exaggeration.

When revealing your "I AM" Humor personality in speeches, use humor to make a point. Then, if the joke bombs, at least you still make the point. If you are used to delivering humor, then don't sweat about when to be funny. Deliver the humorous thoughts as they come to mind. If you did not expect to deliver a joke at a specific point, there is a good chance your audience did not expect it either, and will laugh with you.

Revealing Humor

How do you reveal humor? Do you talk with your face? Consider the clown, revealing humor through the eyes, mouth, and eyebrows. Humor is very physical, and not just in the case of clowns. If you need to dismiss someone, you laugh out and up (tossing your head back), not in and down (tucking your head down). Humor is revealed from the neck up.

Have you ever been told you can't tell a joke? Create a "funny" character as the basis of your "I AM" Humor personality. Use the humor part of the triangle to be funny. Everybody can recognize when something is funny; therefore, everybody can be funny. To reveal humor you need to know the three different flows of energy that run through your body: flying, flowing, and molding.

The way Robin Williams reveals his humor is to make birdlike movements as if he is flying, which is a staccato movement. He's literally flying on stage. Someone who moves in staccato can't stand still. They are constantly in motion. Jenna Elfman, Jim Carrey, Eddie Murphy, and Michael Richards (as Kramer) are flying. Everything is staccato.

Second, there is flowing. Flowing is a legato movement, one that is in an elongated and continuous motion. Jerry Seinfeld is flowing. Everything rolls off his tongue. Charlie Chaplin had flowing, uninterrupted movements as well.

Third is molding. Molding demonstrates the least motion of the three types of energy. Someone who is molding stands in one place, acting as the fulcrum of the energy that they project to the audience. Roseanne is molding, as are Stephen Wright, Louie Anderson, and George Burns.

Try this: model these folks. Make birdlike, staccato movements. Fly in your living room! You'll start talking faster and moving with lightness and ease. Or try flowing in uninterrupted, legato movements. Literally float your body around as you talk and move like you're in a swimming pool. Flowing characters have a sense of style. They flow without tension. Those with tension sink.

Star humor pupils to model:

Robin Williams —*Patch Adams*
Roberto Benigni —*Life is Beautiful*
Whoopi Goldberg —*Sister Act*
Jack Nicholson —*Easy Rider*
Lucille Ball —*I Love Lucy*

Now write down in your journal what type of energy (flying, flowing, or molding) the actors above exhibit.

Feeling Down

Do you ever find times that you feel depressed? Examine the word depressed. What does it mean?

de·pressed (v.)
1. To lower in spirits.
2. To cause to drop or sink; lower.
3. To press down.

Notice the predominant theme in definitions: "To be pushed down." You've heard others say, "I feel so down today," or "I'm feeling low." If you do the exercise below, to promote lightness and ease, I guarantee that you will be physically unable to be depressed.

To be depressed you have to be down, not just mentally and emotionally, but physically as well. With your arms outstretched over your head—there is no way to be completely "down." Seems simple—but try it and feel the difference!

Lightness and Ease

Humor is lightness and ease. You have to be light on your feet. An actor reveals humor through lightness and ease. To philosophize man's struggle since the beginning with the law of gravity, he has always yearned to excel or fly. That is no more apparent to me than when I watch the Olympics. What are the athletes trying to do most of the time? FLY! SOAR! Defy the laws of gravity! The higher they go, the more points they receive. So as an artist armed with the enlightened triangle, everything you do should come with lightness and ease.

ACTING FOR REAL

Raise your hands above your head for 30 seconds and your nervous system will not let you be depressed. Depressed is to be "down." If you are "up," you change your physicality and your emotional state of being. Just as your mood affects your physicality, so can your physicality affect your mood.

Lightness and ease means relaxed muscles, and dynamic light activity. To rise up with lightness and ease, you also have to have fire—remember your heat!

LIGHT AS A FEATHER EXERCISE

Begin by observing the force of gravity pulling you down to the earth. Now, experience elevation by turning your face toward the sky and raising your arms and hands as high as you can reach. Inhale and feel your body filled with air. Do this without any muscle tension. Keep doing this until you are raised up from the earth as much as humanly possible. You will feel as light as a feather, revealing humor with lightness and ease!

Recognize which characters in life represent lightness and ease through their psychological gestures and model them. For example, ministers, politicians, and comedians, constantly have their hands up in the air, gesturing towards the heavens.

So, let's do laughter! Tell someone a funny joke, enjoy life's insanity, smile at your own faults, and laugh with your neighbors. There is no reason a good joke cannot be told more than once. Imagine a conductor refusing to play Beethoven's *Fifth*, on the grounds that someone might have heard it before. Humor is emotional chaos remembered in tranquility.

But most of all ladies and gentlemen, remember—He who laughs last, lasts!

"I AM" Conclusion

You now know how to reveal the three behaviors of the empowered life characters that will drive you to success. When all three of your enlightened "I AM" personalities are portrayed in symphony, complementing one another, revealed with passionate commitment, and in perfect balance, the characters that you play will reflect it. Portraying these personalities is the balance required to meet your specific outcomes—50% of the predominant behavior, with 25% each of the other two—will give you the flexibility and empowerment to win!

The enlightened triangle will tune your instrument with passion, lightness, and fire, the melodious triad that makes the world go around! The harmony of be BOP!

The Dark Triangle Diagram

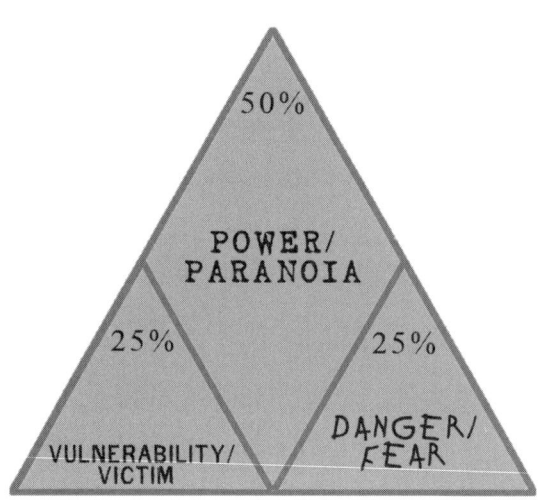

CHAPTER 14
THE DARK TRIANGLE

"Luke, come over to the dark side…"
—Darth Vader

The Dark Triangle

Now let's take a trip over to the shady side of life. Let's talk about the three behaviors in the Creative Wheel that tend to hide in the shadows and occasionally rear their ugly heads to sabotage the enlightened triangle.

The behaviors of the dark triangle compose the three flawed "I AM" personalities—Power, Danger, and Vulnerability. These personalities are constantly battling the enlightened triangle for dominance and strategic positioning. Like your inner critic, their aim is to divert you from any efforts to reach your goals. Although power, danger, and vulnerability are sometimes touted by society as profound and painless roads to instant success, don't be fooled. This is the triangle of imbalance. Many people are initially drawn to the false glamour of the dark triangle—until the truth is revealed.

When I first coach an actor, one of the first things he's dying to work on is revealing his "I AM" Vulnerability character. Does that mean that he has a desire to reveal weakness? Of course he says no, he has a desire to reveal sensitivity. Sensitivity is not in the dark triangle with Vulnerability, it is in the enlightened triangle (in all of the enlightened personalities).

ACTING FOR REAL

The second thing that the actor desires to reveal is his masculinity, which he associates with danger. Is this actor looking for the audience to perceive him as a macho madman? No! He's just trying to find a way to reveal his fiery sexuality. Again, found in the enlightened triangle.

The third thing that the actor desires to reveal is his power. But the "I AM" Power personality, more commonly reveals his paranoia of losing power, than of his ability to gain and maintain real power. Power is the absence of humanities.

When we first start out in life, we all have that fire, and those humanitarian dreams arising from the enlightened triangle. The dark side immediately goes to work trying to entice us with the falsely glamorous images of power, vulnerability, and danger such as paper-thin images of "get rich instantly" and "win quickly with no effort" schemes. Remember, garbage in equals garbage out. Once those images fall, we see the dark side for what it is: paranoia, weakness, and anger.

In order to destroy the flawed dark "I AM" personalities, you must be able to recognize them. It's not as easy as in the old Westerns, where the bad guys always wear black hats. But using your heightened powers of self-awareness, empowered beliefs, your sense of balance, and your enlightened triangle, I'm confident that you will overpower the dark side and win!

POWER

Jan Michael Vincent, Lisa Eilbacher, and Thom in the
1983 miniseries *The Winds of War*

CHAPTER 15
POWER
PARANOIA

*"Not necessity, not desire—no, the love of power is the demon of
men. Let them have everything—health, food, a place to live,
entertainment—they are and remain unhappy and low-spirited: for
the demon waits and waits and will be satisfied."*
                                        —Friedrich Nietzsche

pow·er (n.)
  1. Strength or force exerted or capable of being exerted.
  2. The ability or official capacity to exercise control;
     authority.
  3. A person, group, or nation having great influence or control
     over others.

ACTING FOR REAL

par·a·noi·a (n.)
1. A psychotic disorder characterized by delusions of persecution with or without grandeur, often strenuously defended with apparent logic and reason.
2. Extreme irrational distrust of others.

Power

When I speak of power, I'm not talking about the physical strength of power, the power of existence, or the power of wisdom. I'm talking about the facade of power in everyday life that we chase like the false carrot in front of the ass's nose. The false dream that keeps us moving toward that greedy, selfish, opulent style of life that seems so ideal, ends up creating gaudy architecture, runaway materialism, and a decline in humanitarian values.

Powerful people work out of desperation. The more money they have, the more desperate they become to have more. What jacks them up is not making more money. Paranoia and desperation from a crumbling facade is what motivates power-seeking people.

The "I AM" Power/ Paranoia personality is the dark side of the "I AM" Humanities/ Passion personality. It is the difference between using power to steamroll the path to success, mowing down everyone in our way, versus revealing a passion and love of mankind to reach our goals. Through conditioning, we generally reveal power later in life, out of revenge. People strive for power to "get back" at someone or something that they blame for their negative outcomes. Power is the ultimate way of stepping out of the moment, falling out of balance, and empowering someone else as the cause of your outcomes. The sooner you can understand this and nip it in the bud, the healthier the rest of your life will be. You will not be sucked into power's ugly trap and continuous repercussions.

A good example of this, is the string of dot.com sudden successes, and soon after, dot.com sudden failures in the 1990's. Their accelerated rise to power left these Gen X entrepreneurs with empty vessels and broken dreams. The power of greed created their false sense of security, which very rapidly became their "I AM" Paranoia personality.

Power is well demonstrated in the film *Wall Street* where Michael Douglas's character keeps trying to entice Charlie Sheen's character into the dark side of life where the motto is "greed is good." Unlike in real life, this film had a happy ending—Humanities won!

Another example is in the film *Braveheart*, where Mel Gibson's character fights his power-obsessed enemies with humanities. Once again—the "I AM" Humanities/ Passion character wins. Freedom—from the dark side!

I am not trying to discourage you from revealing power in circumstances where it is required. I do, however, need to show you the dangers of seeking power as a life objective or outcome.

ACTING FOR REAL

Revealing Power

Power can be a positive extension of one's humanities and passion when revealed as an empowering force. For instance, in situations of imminent danger, where a strong assertion of yourself is necessary to avoid harm, power can be revealed.

Assertion should not be confused with aggression. Assertiveness involves standing up for your true rights in a friendly, nonaggressive way. Aggressiveness involves taking advantage of others, causing harm or hurt. Assertiveness should also not be confused with passivity. Passivity is unpleasant. It is meekness, not standing up for what you believe in. It is doing nothing. Yet in doing nothing, you are still choosing to do something that will effect your outcomes. Assertiveness is the balance between passivity and aggression and should be your option when choosing to reveal power.

To reveal power as an assertive, empowering force, square up, lean forward, ask for a lot of options, and give none. The psychological gesture for power is extending your hand upright in front of you. With that gesture, you are saying: "Hold it," "Stop right there pal!" and "Let's discuss our options." Give it a try!

Here is another good example of where power can be used positively. When the "I AM" Sexuality/ Desire personality runs into trouble (the fire burns out of control), it is the perfect time to use the psychological gesture of power, as described above, to protect yourself. Square up, ask for many options, and give none!

How do you reveal power? Fill in the blanks.

By _____up, _____ forward, asking for
_____, and giving _____.

Find the answers by re-reading the text above.

Power is good if you understand it and learn how to control it without craving it and, ultimately, becoming addicted to it. If Power/ Paranoia is one of the "I AM" personalities that has been driving you toward your outcomes (be honest now), let's shine a light on it right now!

Paranoia

The other dark side of the "I AM" Humanities/ Passion personality is Paranoia. The rhythm of paranoia is staccato—think Woody Allen's characters. It may be fun for us, as the audience, to laugh at these neurotic goofballs. But in real life, people reveal paranoia through very unfunny means: hypochondria, anxiety, and mental angst. It's not funny at all to them.

How do we break out of this personality? By going back to the enlightened triangle, of course! Lighten up! There's always a cure for the dark if you turn on the light!

If you find yourself in the shadows of paranoia, go back to the Lightness and Ease Exercise and defy the gravity that is pulling you down into your paranoid state. Notice how similar the body positioning of a paranoid person is to a depressed person—down and hunched forward.

Paranoia occurs when your attention and your "heat" are scattered outside of yourself, rendering them virtually useless. Revealing the behaviors of the enlightened triangle will center your attention back within yourself and help you to regain your balance.

Use lightness and ease to unfold back into your "enlightened" body position. Revisit humor and health to get your balance back. Change the rhythm of your life from staccato to legato—yoga, tai chi, and other relaxation techniques can help put you back into the natural, flowing, artistic rhythm of life.

The Stoke Your Fire Exercise will rekindle and channel the fire within you. Take charge of yourself again with passion and energy. Get involved! Stop being a taker and start giving back. This will take you out of a paranoid state, and put you back in the driver's seat of your "I AM" Humanities personality!

Like a vampire—the most feared enemy of the dark triangle is the light.

VULNERABILITY
Thom tripping in a cowboy shooting in the 1968 film
Hot Spur

CHAPTER 16
VULNERABILITY
VICTIM

"The acknowledgment of our weakness is the first step in repairing our loss."

—*Thomas A. Kempis*

"You cannot run away from weakness; you must some time fight it out or perish; and if that be so, why not now, and where you stand?"

—*Robert Louis Stevenson*

vulner·a·bili·ty (n.)
1. Open to criticism or attack.
2. Easily hurt, as by adverse criticism; sensitive.

vic·tim (n.)
1. Someone or something killed, destroyed, injured, or otherwise harmed by, or suffering from, some act, condition, or circumstance.

The "I AM" Vulnerability/ Victim personality is the most well cast character in our society. Over 80% of people cast the victim character as the primary "I AM" personality in their life, "Woe is me!, It's not my fault!, Why me?" Feeling sorry for yourself has nearly become an art form in our society today. From eating disorders to substance abuse, this "I AM" personality can be found everywhere.

I've found through my coaching that most actors perceive vulnerability as somehow sexy, and sensitive, akin to James Dean, Marilyn Monroe, and Montgomery Clift. Ironically, these actors all died young. Suddenly vulnerability doesn't seem so sexy. In reality, the sensitivity associated with vulnerability leaves actors raw, revealing weakness, and open for attack.

If you've cast yourself as this character in life, here's what you need to do to find the light. You need to find your funny zone and laugh at yourself, find a way to reveal your humanities, and rekindle your passion for life. Sound familiar? Use the behaviors of the enlightened triangle to change the characters you play from weak to empowered. From dark to light!

Vulnerability/ Victim

An actor covers vulnerability by creatively hiding. You can do the same thing! Find ways to cover your vulnerability character with your "I AM" Humanities/ Passion, Humor/ Health, and Sexuality/ Desire personalities. Remember when you were passionate about life as a child and sought to make a difference in this world? Give back at least one hour a month to a humanitarian cause (charity, volunteer work) to stoke your inner fire!

By continuing to cover your "I AM" Vulnerability/ Victim personality with enlightened behaviors, you will eventually kill your inner victim character and portray exclusively enlightened characters in your life. Your inner critic will become the victim of your enlightenment!

DANGER

Thom preparing for a jump on his dirt bike

CHAPTER 17
DANGER
FEAR

dan·ger (n.)
1. Exposure or vulnerability to harm or risk.
2. A source or an instance of risk or peril.
3. Having the power to harm oneself or others.

"I AM" Danger/ Fear Personality

What happens when we are confronted with a sudden and unexpected danger? It would seem that the physiological necessity of coping with whatever is threatening us would make us breathe more rapidly in order to oxygenate our muscles, and indeed, when the initial shock has worn off, our fear is expressed by rapid and shallow panting. But our initial reaction at the time of the first shock is just the opposite: we take a sudden breath, quickly shut our mouths, and then hold the breath in for a period of time. It is as if we are saying to the outside world, "You threaten me; you can't come in. I'm closing the door to you."

The primary mechanism of the "I AM" Danger/ Fear personality is breathing. The most basic body movement pattern is that of a single breath. The triad of a single breath starts with a period of rising tension (inhaling), continues into a crisis (a momentary holding of the breath), and ends with a release (exhaling).

ACTING FOR REAL

To demonstrate this reaction, let's pretend we're in danger. Take a breath in a way that releases its full dramatic potential. Involve your entire body in the rise, crisis, and release triad. Imagine your starting point as an empty balloon. Now inhale to a high crisis and hold it, prolong the crisis, feeling the full strength of the held-back energy. Now release completely. Let it all out!

"Anger is one letter short of danger."
　　　　　　　　　　　—Unknown

As you were holding your breath, did you notice the same behavior or posture that you reveal when you are angry (i.e. executing danger) or in a dangerous situation? If not, then remember a time when you got angry and your mother told you to breathe. Count to ten and breathe!

Once you understand this mechanism, it is no longer automatic. It is a tool that YOU are in control of in danger situations. The actors that I work with agree that the most effective tool that exists for the communication and expression of emotion is controlling your breathing.

I have observed the importance of controlled breathing in all areas of life, not just acting and not just in danger situations. In fact, a powerful way of avoiding danger situations is by building trust and rapport with those around you. Pacing a person's breathing (controlling your own breathing to match someone else's breathing exactly) is the most powerful method of building rapport. Breathing controls a person's internal state to a large degree.

rapport. Breathing controls a person's internal state to a large degree.

Pacing a person's breathing gives you a powerful way of building rapport with someone's internal emotional state. In a danger situation, pacing the other person's tonality brings you into rapport with them, so you can lead them out of danger and back to the enlightened triangle.

Duplicating Danger/ Fear

We as humans are always drawn to dangerous characters. Like the girl who is always attracted to the bad boy—in showbiz, we call him the "antihero" (Alan Ladd, John Garfield, Bruce Willis, Brad Pitt, etc.).

Danger Role Models:

Clint Eastwood —"Make my day."
Robert DeNiro —"You lookin' at me?"
Arnold Schwarzenegger —"I'll be back!"
Jack Nicholson —"Heeerre's Johnny!"

What do all these Hollywood characters have in common? The actors portraying them understand how to reveal the behavior and posturing of the "I AM" Danger/ Fear personality. They are simply duplicating the psychological gesture of controlled breathing, just as you learned above.

ACTING FOR REAL

Now that you are aware of how danger manifests itself, you are in control of this personality too. Danger is no longer an unknown variable to be feared. Remember what Mom said, "Count to ten, and take a few good deep breaths."

Dark Triangle Summary

In all the great books, religious, philosophical, and otherwise, there is always a battle between the enlightenment and darkness that struggle for power within you. Through increased knowledge and self-awareness, you will be able to shine light onto your dark side that will allow you to become increasingly empowered by gradually transforming the dark into light. Through your awareness and ability to control the behaviors of the dark triangle, you now have the tools to accomplish this life-changing transformation. Shine on!

CHAPTER 18
THE CREATIVE WHEEL WRAP-UP

"Personality is only ripe when a man has made the truth his own."
—*Søren Kierkegaard*

All styles of drama reveal the psychology of life through physical behavior. The genius of the actor is that he can duplicate life using specific behaviors and characters, as are found in the Creative Wheel. An actor becomes an actor either because he craves to exploit his own personality, or the very opposite. He may, and many actors do, have a need to become a variety of characters.

I divide actors into two categories: personality actors and transformers. The transformer actor literally transforms himself into the character he is playing, while the personality actor bases the character he is playing on his own "I AM" personality. Although you may not immediately see which category you belong in, keep reading and working on yourself and you will find out after a short period of exploration.

There are very few actors who fit into both groups. The personality actor is the one we enjoy seeing cast to type. The actor for whom we go to the movies to see portray himself, such as Tom Hanks, Jim Carrey, Eddie Murphy, Robin Williams, Julia Roberts, Harrison Ford, and Tom Cruise. If he strays outside his own "I AM" personality and plays a part outside of his essence, we are disappointed in him. The personality actor's strongest tool in creating a character is his own "I AM" personality and all of its behaviors and nuances.

The actors who play different personalities—Sean Penn, Dustin Hoffman, Denzel Washington, Gwyneth Paltrow, Billy Bob Thornton, Cate Blanchett, Robert DeNiro, Halle Berry, Meryl Streep, Russell Crowe—are called transformers. We watch with surprise, rather than familiarity, as they reveal a completely different triangle of "I AM" personalities in each role that they play. This is not simply a question of makeup or wardrobe. These actors learn to duplicate vastly different behaviors in order to portray such diverse characters completely different from themselves. Transformer actors have a thorough understanding of the psychology of each of the behaviors of the Creative Wheel, and how to duplicate them.

Neither type of actor can convince the audience of anything merely through his outward appearance (makeup, costume, etc.), just as no layperson can convince you of anything merely by his outward appearance. A wolf is still a wolf, even if it is in sheep's clothing. Costume and makeup are simply the final touches in conveying the character that the actor has created to the audience.

I had a conversation with the late, great, Sir Laurence Olivier once, while his son was studying in Southern California and Sir Laurence was living in Los Angeles. When speaking about the craft of acting, he pointed out to me the major difference between the English and American processes of working on characters.

He said,

"American actors are lazy because they don't work on themselves and therefore, their characters, at all. English actors work on parts for five to ten years."

The way he worked on a part was that he never saw himself as the character. The first thing that he would do would be to visualize the character as he read the material, many times, never once seeing himself in the character's circumstance. It was his job as the actor to create that character. He never heard his own voice as the character. He would find the character's voice and duplicate that. He wasn't interested in feeling as the character; he was only interested in filling the character with the period, setting, and atmosphere. Olivier would create the character in his mind, as the author had created him on paper. He would create the character, like a builder would build a house, and then step into it.

So he was the type of transformer actor who, during rehearsals, loses himself in the character's "I AM" personality. Like Olivier, by the time of the performance, the actor has already accepted himself as the character he is portraying and would be surprised if a mirror were placed in front of him.

As the story goes, when Sean Penn got his big break playing the character Jeff Spicoli in *Fast Times at Ridgemont High*, the young actor wouldn't respond to any other name during filming. At one point, he even insisted on being locked in Spicoli's bedroom overnight, which of course, was nothing more than a movie set with props. His belief was that he WAS that character, instead of his own "I AM" personality.

In other words, we're not really aware of who we are, the personality actor or the transformer, until the process of self-exploration that we've detailed so far in this book, reveals it to us. In order to know, we must start with understanding the Creative Triangle and core "I AM" personalities that we portray every day. Know thyself!

The Creative Wheel of Behavior is your foundation for all of the characters you will play in life. You now have the circle of characters to cast yourself as the star in your life. You have the power to identify the ones that you are currently portraying, and create new, enlightened characters that you will portray to reach your goals. Now let's put the wheel to work for you, the Actor for Real!

CHAPTER 19
CREATING EMPOWERED CHARACTERS

"Now what else is the whole life of mortals but a sort of comedy, in which the various actors, disguised by various costumes and masks, walk on and play each one his part, until the manager waves them off the stage..."
                                                    —*Erasmus*

"We are a kind of Chameleons, taking our hue... from those who are about us."
                                                    —*John Locke*

"You cannot dream yourself into a character; you must hammer and forge yourself one."
                                                    —*James A. Froude*

If you don't like your own character, there may be a new one ready-made and waiting for you. The snake sheds its dead skin, using the same methods you can use.

Acting is reverse engineering. A professional actor is given a product by a writer and must dismantle it, study it, and then put it back together, revealing a bit of that character at a time. Acting is not talking—acting is doing. And the things you do, you do because something exists to make you do it. Character comes from the way you do a thing. The doing is basic. The way you do it may vary. As your reasons change, your character changes.

Now that you've dismantled and studied the six "I AM" personalities of the Creative Wheel of Behavior, it's time to mold them into your new empowered life character. Are you ready for your close-up?

First, you will identify the enlightened personalities that you are currently portraying and learn how to incorporate them with passion into your daily life. The enlightened triangle (Humanities/ Passion, Humor/ Health, Sexuality/ Desire) is the foundation for all of your empowered characters. Next, you will learn to nuke any negative behaviors that you portray (Power/ Paranoia, Vulnerability/ Victim, and Danger/ Fear). The dark triangle acts as a stop for all of your positive outcomes. Finally, and most importantly, you'll learn how to adapt and flex your new character to succeed in any situation that life throws at you! You'll be a professional surfer, skillfully riding the waves, and continuously making small adjustments in your character so that you're always in perfect balance on the path to your goals.

Build Strength Where Strength Lies

HUMANITIES/ PASSION

How can you identify the "I AM" Humanities/ Passion personality that you are already portraying and heighten it? Remember the importance of self-observation and ask yourself questions. Get out your journal and answer these questions in as much depth as possible. Your answers will reveal the intensity of your "I AM" Humanities personality.

What have you given back to humanity?

Are you involved in making this world a better place?

How involved are you in our society?

Are you involved in charity?

Are you active in your religion/ spirituality?

How are you rekindling your passion for life daily?

Roll back time to when you were driven to change the world. You knew in your heart that giving back to humanity was the right thing to do, and felt you had the ability and courage to do it! Now, make a list of everything that has happened to you between then and now. Why don't you have that level of passion anymore? What are you going to do TODAY to start rekindling it?

Pick up litter when you see it lying on the road, and by all means, don't contribute to it! Lead by example. Find a cause you are passionate about and get involved. Are you passionate about politics, animals, world hunger, homelessness? Find a group you can get involved with. There are so many to choose from, and some require very little time commitments. Help out on a build for Habitat for Humanity one weekend. Send a check and a letter every month to help a child in a third world country. Volunteer to instruct a youth group. Or join a local animal welfare chapter. If organizations out there don't appeal to you, start your own! There is so much you can do to ignite your passions, and not only will it empower you, it will empower others as well. You will be rewarded in ways you never thought. By being involved, you lift yourself up. You gain self-respect and you gain a proud sense of accomplishment. You also inspire others and a ripple effect occurs. All the good that you put out spreads and is communicable. Inevitably, it will all come back full circle to you, and you can pass it on again.

SEXUALITY/ DESIRE

Who are you in the realm of your "I AM" Sexuality/Desire personality? Identify a movie character that, as soon as you saw them on the screen, you instantly admired for their natural sexuality that they revealed. Now, compare yourself with that character and write down your answers to these questions in your journal.

> Who are you in relation to that character (their love interest, best friend, jealous rival, an extra in the background, the undesirable co-star, etc.)?
>
> What does the leading lady/ man have that you do not have?
>
> Which behaviors do you need to learn to duplicate to get what they have?

Talent is knowledge. Do you see yourself as others see you? If you were on the dating game—would you be chosen and why? Make a case for yourself:

Why should I choose you?

Which of the bachelors/ bachelorettes are you attracted to?

What kind of people are you generally drawn to sexually? Who do you desire?

Why are you drawn to these people?

What do they have in their store to offer you?

Now, create a profile of your soul mate. Write down 10 things he or she has that you desire (physical appearance, personality, interests, etc.). By identifying your soul mate, you're identifying the perfect reflection of the "I AM" Sexuality personality that YOU desire to portray. You will identify the character YOU are playing, by identifying the character that is the ideal reflection of you.

Would your soul mate be interested in you? Why or why not?

If not, what can you change about yourself to make that happen?

What characters do you need to create to make them attracted to you?

YOU are a work in progress. When you can look in the mirror and feel great, you will be empowered to reach all the goals that you set for yourself. You will be a good Actor for Real, portraying a real enlightened personality!

ACTING FOR REAL

HUMOR/ HEALTH

Now, let's shine a light on your "I AM" Humor/Health personality. When you nurture and heighten this personality, you are buying a ticket to life! You already know that humor is the most important thing for your health. My late mother, at the age of 86, may have been weak physically, but her mind was great—all because of her sense of humor.

Your sense of humor also strengthens the rest of your enlightened triangle. When it comes to relationships, communication, humor, and sexuality are the keys to making them successful. And when you are healthy and happy, it will be even easier to rekindle your passion for humanities.

How can you assess the state of your "I AM" Humor personality? Well, if you're reading this from your hospital bed with a stress ulcer and high blood pressure, chances are this personality needs a lot of work! Even if you're not, the majority of us tend to take the "more important" aspects of life so seriously, that humor gets swept to the wayside. When you finally understand the vital connection between your sense of humor and health, you will make this "I AM" personality one of your top three priorities, along with humanities and sexuality.

Now, it's time for your checkup! Write down the answers to these questions in your journal:

What kind of humor do you like?
What makes you laugh?
Do you make yourself laugh?
Do you laugh at yourself?
What kind of comedian are you? Flying, flowing, or molding?
Which actors can you model to build strength in your type of humor?
What made you laugh today? Why?

Keep a journal of what makes you really laugh (belly laughs) and seek it out daily! If you go more than two days without finding anything to laugh at, then you need to get serious about humor!

Create a "joke club" with your family and friends where you can exchange jokes, stories, and humor freely. Get the courage to tell a story, a joke: Do people laugh? If not, analyze the physical behaviors and postures that you used. Find role models to copy to get better ones. Now you are closer to understanding how to reveal your sense of humor!

A Work in Progress

How will you know when your enlightened personality is at its peak? You won't! You are a work in progress, and your enlightened personalities will grow and strengthen, every day, for the rest of your life. Your aim is to constantly work on them, rekindle them, and find ways to portray them in everything you do.

In the meantime, you can reveal where you stand by continuously observing yourself in all three areas: Humanities/

Passion, Sexuality/ Desire, and Humor/ Health. What are the pictures you're seeing of yourself? Have someone take a series of pictures of you or shoot a movie. Then start analyzing the pictures and see what you would like to change. Look at your postures, facial expressions, and level of passion.

You'll never know how well you're doing, until you start observing yourself every day, in every way. You must do this ALL day, not just at night in front of the mirror, but in each moment of your day, all the time. When you are in a constant state of self-observation, you will constantly be assessing yourself and making positive, empowering changes.

Once you start out on the road to enlightenment, and plant the statement in your conscious mind, "We're going to make changes!" your inner critic will eventually kick in. It will state, "We'll get him—he'll become *casual* eventually!" Unfortunately, this is generally true when most people attempt positive change in their lives. They get "casual," and all good intentions set in place at the beginning of the process are lost. You must not be casual! You must be constantly vigilant and observant! Always observing and making changes! Once you become casual, you will become the victim of your inner critic. Casualness is what gets us! If you notice yourself becoming casual, reread the chapters in this book to get you back on track!

Casualness = Casualty

Intentions are useless if they are not attached to constant vigilance and ACTION! Does that mean you have to be "on" all the time? Yes! If you desire to make lasting, positive changes—YES! Now, let's nuke the negative personalities that are working with your inner critic to bring down the enlightened character that you just worked so hard to create.

Nuke the Negative

It's time to identify and "nuke" the negative behaviors that you are currently portraying. Take out your journal and read your answers to the questions in the previous section, where you assessed your enlightened "I AM" personalities. If you are not satisfied with the intensity of your enlightened behaviors, then you are portraying one or more of the dark personalities: Danger, Vulnerability, and Power. Now, how do you know which personalities of the dark triangle you are portraying?

Power

Answer these questions honestly, in your journal:

Do you find that you are constantly checking your back?

Are you afraid that nobody is looking out for you—except you?

ACTING FOR REAL

Do you consistently devise strategies to win your outcomes that require you to take something away from someone, or somehow harm other people?

Do you take actions to help other people, or strictly for personal gain?

Does a wave of paranoia kick in at least once a day?

Do you believe that any success you have is on borrowed time?

Now, write a eulogy for yourself describing what you have achieved so far in your life. Analyze who you hurt and what you took from others, or destroyed to reach this point in your life. Write another one that analyzes your selfless sacrifices, how you gave to others, and what obstacles you overcame to reach this point in life. Read each eulogy and decide which person it is you desire to be and build on those positive characteristics while nuking the negative ones. Have you ever known someone who passed away and no one volunteered to do the eulogy because no one had anything nice to say? Don't be one of those people!

Rekindle your passion for life. Give at least one to two hours a month to some humanitarian organization to empower the universe. Get involved. Do nice things on a regular basis: open a door for a stranger, help an old lady across the street, clean up your food tray at the mall, throw away your own popcorn at the movies, yield to pedestrians and other vehicles.

Find something in your store that when you share it with others, will help them. *Sharing* and *caring* nuke the paranoia! Identify what you're paranoid about. Learn to give of yourself. Give without expecting anything in return. Paranoia comes from not wanting to share—fearing that you'll be taken advantage of. Once you start sharing unconditionally, you will no longer be paranoid about being taken advantage of.

You create your own reality by what you believe—positive and negative. What you believe WILL be your reality. When you realize that you are on a journey, and the only way to succeed is by giving instead of simply taking, then the character you create and your accomplishments will be everlasting.

The Paranoid Character

Everybody starts life with the idea that they'll change the world. They'll make the world a better place. Then you become successful, but instead of changing the world, you begin to crave power. This power quickly becomes paranoia. You become more concerned with other people's success and how it impacts your own success. Thus, the more power the character has, the more paranoid he becomes. Howard Hughes was famously paranoid. He wouldn't even shake your hand. Politicians become paranoid. Look at Nixon. When you understand that power is a negative component of the triangle, you'll stop the paranoia. You'll turn that energy to passion and humanities. If you're full of passion about something, you've replaced the paranoid aspect of power and become truly powerful. Look at Mother Teresa, Ghandi. Ted

ACTING FOR REAL

Turner became "bigger" in most people's eyes when he gave a billion dollars to charity. He stopped being a mogul and became someone who's doing something to change the world. He transformed his dark power character into an enlightened humanitarian.

The Victim Character

If you find yourself playing the blame game—"she did it, I didn't do it, it wasn't my fault!"—you will think that you are always being acted upon, being taken advantage of, not appreciated. You will not be interested in even starting to make changes in your life because it will seem too painful. How many times in a week do you avoid responsibility for your actions and blame it on someone else? If you observe that in yourself, go back, capture that mental snapshot of where, when, and why it happened. If you had the opportunity, how would you turn that situation around to benefit everybody? What enlightened personality could you portray in that situation—which personality or behavior would you substitute? Humanities? Humor? Sexuality? Roll back time and pick a major crash in your life (a failure, something that stopped you from pursuing a dream, stopped moving you forward toward an outcome—a failed purpose). Identify everything that has happened as a result of that stop. How have you stopped moving forward not only toward the outcome you were pursuing at the time, but how has it crossed over and affected your actions towards other outcomes? The wonderful thing about when you are only competing against yourself is, you can observe how you are holding yourself back. Why give 110% when I'm going to fail anyway? The best way to correct the victim character is to validate the accomplishments you have made. Do you ever hear yourself whining, uttering a peevish, high-pitched, somewhat nasal sound as in complaint, distress, or fear? Listen to the way you respond about challenges that life presents you. Observe your body. Are you out of balance? Check your body language. Is your head hanging down? Are you groomed? Do you smell? Have you lost your pride in your appearance? Some are so afraid of others, they are convinced that disaster will befall them at any moment. So they prepare themselves for it rather than preparing for success. They may never give anything back to anyone else, halting what would otherwise create positive changes in their own life. It makes them personally weak, as they never receive the rewards and adulations of giving. "I hardly have anything, so why should I give to other people who all seem to be doing better than me already?" Generosity breeds generosity and effects all outcomes in life.

"Those who whine—will never dine with the classes."
—Thom McFadden

"Winners don't whine and whiners don't win."
—Thom McFadden

ACTING FOR REAL

Stop the Victim

Validate yourself for all your accomplishments. Take responsibility for your actions instead of blaming them on others. Take small steps towards your desired outcomes and validate each one. Stay in BOP—observe your body, how you walk, your physical appearance (grooming)—take pride in how you look, what you do, how you do it, how you talk, etc. Keep an eye on yourself and stop making excuses. Stop the blame game. Take responsibility for your outcomes and you will feel deserving of the effects. Responsibility for your actions equals responsibility for your successes.

Danger: Extroverted

Are you a time bomb waiting to explode? Do you hold your breath a lot? Do you have a short fuse? Do you find yourself exploding and lashing out quickly? Have you lost control of your anger? Are you unable to cope with the slightest challenge, tension, or anxiety? Have you turned your stress into anger? Do you work through stressful situations or just stew in them?

Danger: Introverted

The ulcer personality: cautious, temperate. Do you bottle up your anxiety and never let it out until you have a heart attack? Do you have road rage? It is thought that the most timid personalities drive SUVs. Are you a drunk or a druggie? Do you have an addictive personality? Do you have medical conditions such as: GI distress, heartburn, high blood pressure? Do you release pent up frustration with sudden violence? Are you explosively dangerous to others? Do you have physical ailments? Do you binge on food, alcohol, substances, gambling or porn?

Lower your expectations by 25% of what you're expecting from the target of your anger. For example: If you are in the fast lane and you drive up behind someone going slower than you (a dangerous situation), find the humor in the situation. Find a way to cope. Breathe. Take 10 long, deep breaths. By slowing and relaxing your body through breathing, you calm your body and mind. You can't stay angry or scared if you're breathing. Concentrate. Oxygen to your brain helps you think clearly. A person full of rage is not thinking clearly. Try other helpful coping mechanisms such as exercise, yoga, or hiking. Regular exercise strengthens your body and mind. And don't forget humor, the best coping mechanism for most danger/ fear/ anger situations. Laughing also brings oxygen to your brain and is contagious.

Creating "Style" For Yourself

To make change, there must be a realization that you desire change. You desire outcomes. Stoke that fire! Don't be casual! Feed your desire! Feed the fire in your veins and let it propel you towards your outcomes. That desire will allow you to step into the arena. How do you do that? Portray the enlightened character that you create. Each small win will build upon another, creating larger wins. Become the character. Start small. Each win is significant. Come up with a plan (Act III) and climb the ladder.

Wants, Needs, Desires

Make your *needs* your desires, and all your *wants* will come true. Needs are driven by passion. Wants are superficial whims. Wants are to needs, as a melancholy gasp of air is to essential breathing. When you need something, you are driven to get it. When you want something, you wait for it to come along. Don't just *want* something—*need* it! Just as our thoughts are first a picture in our mind of our desired outcomes, our actions are conducted by the power of our words. *Speak* like a driven, enlightened personality, *act* like a driven, enlightened personality, *be* a driven, enlightened personality!

Observe life. Read books. Go to concerts. Go to museums. Stare! See someone at the bank who is portraying a specific enlightened behavior. Identify the behavior. Play it back in your mind and put it to use based on your knowledge from these chapters. Then duplicate it!

Create a need in your life to find personal coaches/ mentors to be objective for you and see you as others see you. If you had one week to live, what changes would you make today? What character would you start portraying today? Start working on one little thing (a want, a need or a desire) at a time, EVERY DAY. Which are you most passionate about at this time? Let it fuel you to make the change.

Downtime

To connect with a character's intellectual center, or source point, an actor gathers information about the character that is analogous to him or herself. By getting out of one's own self, one can observe the character without judgment. Only then can the character become explored without emotional involvement. Throughout this process, the actor will discover how to reveal the behaviors needed to portray a full dimensional character. This process is called "downtime."

As an actor during downtime, you must get out of your own way and avoid bringing the character down to your limited "I AM" personality. Don't let yourself be a stop in the way of your character. Don't get so emotionally involved that you're not able to see the tree before the forest.

We often refer to movie characters as "larger than life." In reality, it is life that is large. You must rise to the occasion by portraying characters that are larger than life. You must multiply who you are to a very large, heightened character in a given circumstance. We miniaturize ourselves with a lack of knowledge, stops, or fears, by feeding our inner critic, limiting our beliefs, and ignoring our senses. You, as the Actor for Real, must rise to your empowered life character instead of bringing the character down to you. When you are working on creating your Acting for Real characters, self-exploration is your downtime.

Uptime

What is uptime? It is your will's impulse. Uptime is performing the personalities that you have created during downtime. It is the execution of the character that the actor has developed during downtime. You've heard of "shooting the scene" in Hollywood… uptime for the Actor for Real is taking the character you've created during your downtime and putting it into action!

Putting Characters into ACTION!

There's a popular phrase that states, "Fake it 'til you make it." When you create a new character, especially an emotional one, at first you may have to "fake" the external characteristics of the character until they finally come naturally to you. This is where you will employ the "magic if" that you learned earlier in this book.

For example, in acting, when an actor is required to cry in a role and has trouble turning on the waterworks, he should fake the tears. Even though the tears aren't there, he should fight them back, as if they were. This may sound like an example of amateur night at the local theater, but it is actually a better choice than exhibiting your frustration with yourself at not being able to cry, and damaging the rest of your performance.

Once you identify the enlightened behaviors that make up your new empowered, characters, duplicate the behaviors that you learned in the last chapter and practice them daily! Play pretend, and above all, don't beat yourself up if the process doesn't come easily to you. It won't at first, but if you keep duplicating the behaviors, your new character will soon feel completely natural and organic. In other words, rehearse, rehearse, rehearse, and you will be an actor…for real!

ACTION!

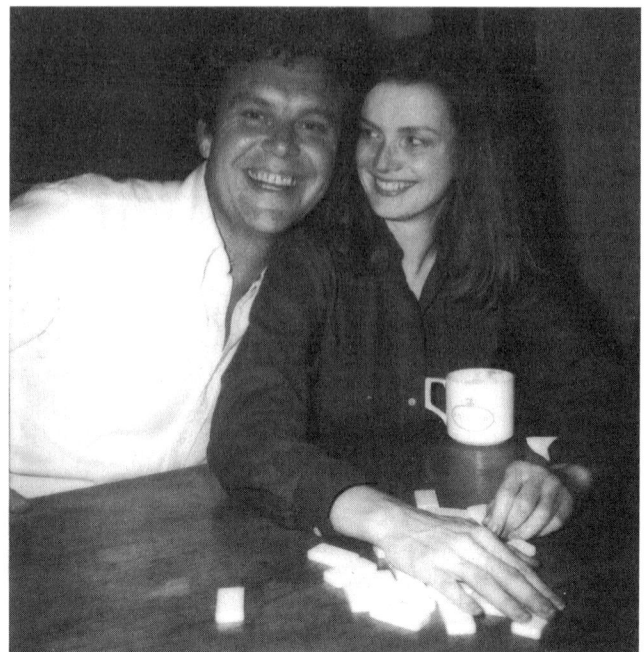

Thom with actress Blair Brown, star of the TV
series *The Days and Nights of Molly Dodd*

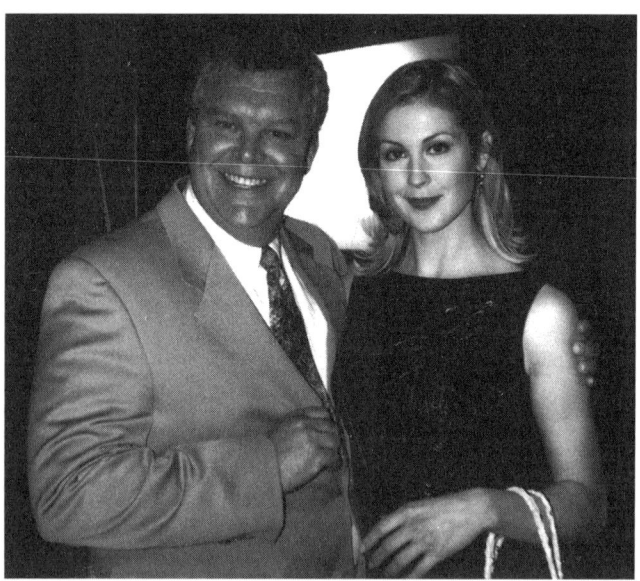

Thom with Kelly Rutherford on the set of *Melrose Place*
TV drama series

Tom Selleck and Thom on the set of *Magnum P.I.*
TV series

Thom with Dorothy Tristan on the set of the 1979
film *California Dreaming*

ACTING FOR REAL

John Murray and Thom on the set of *Moving Violations*

Thom, Nedra Volz, and Fred Willard on the set of
Moving Violations

ACTING FOR REAL

Tim Matheson and Thom

Thom and Larry Pisoni, famous clown and founder of
Pickle Family Circus

The founders of the American Children's Theater: Thom, child star Evelyn Rudie, and husband Chris DeCarlo

Westside Repertory Theater Troup—*the X-Rated Players*—Christmas Party with artistic director and acting coach Thom, in center, and wife, Nancy, to his right

Thom and Nancy's three sons

Will, actor, and Tyler and James, co-founders, writers/
producers and directors of GoPotato.tv

Act THREE

THE ACTOR FOR REAL'S TOOLBOX

CHAPTER 20
CREATIVE VISUALIZATION

"The subconscious mind does not know the difference between an actual experience and a vividly imagined one."
                                        —Dennis Waitley

REMEMBERING THE PAST EXERCISE

Sit for a period of at least one hour, alone. Relax all your muscles. Allow your associations to proceed but do not be absorbed by them. Say to them, "If you will let me do as I wish now, I shall later grant your wishes." Negotiate with your inner critic! Look on your associations as though they belonged to someone else. See yourself, to keep yourself from identifying with them.

At the end of the hour, take a piece of paper and write your aim on it. Make this paper your outcome—be possessed! Everything else is nothing. Take it out of your pocket and read it constantly, every day. In this way it becomes a part of you, at first theoretically, later, actually. To gain energy, practice this exercise of sitting still and relaxing your muscles. Only when everything within you is quiet, make your decision about your aim. Don't let associations absorb you. To undertake a voluntary aim, and to achieve it, gives magnetism and the ability "to do."

Major James Nesmeth had a dream of improving his golf game and he developed a unique method of achieving his goal. Until he devised this method, he was just your average weekend golfer, shooting in the mid-to-low '90s. Then, for seven years, he completely quit the game. Never touched a club. Never set foot on a fairway.

ACTING FOR REAL

Ironically, it was during this seven-year break from the game that Major Nesmeth came up with his amazing technique for improving his game, a technique we can all learn from. In fact, the first time he set foot on a golf course after his hiatus from the game, he shot an astonishing 74! He had cut 20 strokes off his average without having ever swung a golf club in 7 years! Unbelievable! Not only that, but his physical condition had actually deteriorated during those seven years.

What was Major Nesmeth's secret? Visualization.

You see, Major Nesmeth had spent those seven years as a prisoner of war in North Vietnam. During those seven years, he was imprisoned in a cage that was approximately four-and-a-half feet high and five feet long.

During almost the entire time he was imprisoned, he saw no one, talked to no one and experienced no physical activity. During the first few months he did virtually nothing but hope and pray for his release. Then he realized he had to find some way to occupy his mind or he would lose his sanity and probably his life. That's when he learned to visualize.

In his mind, he selected his favorite golf course and started playing golf. Every day, he played a full 18 holes at the imaginary country club of his dreams. He experienced everything down to the last detail. He saw himself dressed in his golfing clothes. He smelled the fragrance of the trees and the freshly trimmed grass.

He experienced different weather conditions—windy spring days, overcast winter days, and sunny summer mornings. In his imagination, every detail of the tee, the individual blades of grass, the trees, the singing birds, the scampering squirrels, and the lay of the course became totally real.

He felt the grip of the club in his hands. He instructed himself as he practiced smoothing out his downswing and the follow-through on his shot. Then he watched the ball arc down the exact center of the fairway, bounce a couple of times and roll to the exact spot he had selected, all in his mind.

In the real world, he was in no hurry. He had no place to go. So in his mind he took every step on his way to the ball, just as if he were physically on the course. It took him just as long in imaginary time to play 18 holes as it would have taken in reality. Not a detail was omitted. Not once did he ever miss a shot, never a hook or slice, never a missed putt.

Seven days a week. Four hours a day. Eighteen holes. Seven years. Twenty strokes off. Shot a 74!

Wow! The power of visualization! How do you envision your future? Is it what you are living now?

Visualization requires not only the visual sense, but the auditory, olfactory, kinesthetic senses and sense of taste, as well. What you visualize and focus on manifests itself. When you do this with specificity, and an intense desire, you hasten the process. If you visualize a property that is not in the present, and you visualize it as having occurred, and you behave as if it were real, thoroughly enjoying it, you are turning yourself into a magnet, a tool that will turn that event into a reality! When coaching actors, I have them visualize standing on the stage and hearing the applause of the crowd as they bow.

The strategy of focused imagery and creative visualization is a technique for using your imagination to create what you desire in life.

WHAT YOU PROJECT IN YOUR MIND AND THINK ABOUT WITH GREAT PASSION AND EMOTION COMES INTO BEING

The key to creative visualization and focused imagery is visualizing exactly and precisely your future as you would like it to be. Leave nothing to chance.

Everything should be in the exact detail that you desire to achieve. See it, hear it, feel it, smell it, taste it. Then, recognize that the object in your mind, your desired and intended future, is in the present, and that you are currently enjoying that state. You must clearly define and project in your mind what you desire. Do so with passion that emotionalizes the desired object and outcome. You must consider it as already accomplished. When you have mastered this process, your desired future will come.

In the past, many of us have used our power of creative visualization in an unconscious way. Because of deep-seated negative beliefs about life, we have automatically and unconsciously expected and visualized limitations, difficulties, and problems in our lives. It is very easy to create the negative outcomes we visualize.

Learn to use your natural creative imagination in a positive and conscious way to create what you truly wish for, whether it's love, enjoyment, etc. Daydream it into reality. The use of creative visualization follows the scientific reality that all desired outcomes are first a picture of our thoughts. Imagination is the ability to create an idea or mental picture in your mind. In creative visualization, you will use your imagination to create an image of something you wish to achieve. Then, you continue to regularly focus on the idea, giving it positive energy and great passion, and consider it already accomplished. With this strategy, your objective becomes a reality much sooner.

After relaxing, visualize what you truly desire. Create the feeling that your mental image is possible. Experience it as if it is already happening. Repeat this exercise two or three times each and every day.

Creative visualization is a science in the truest and highest meaning of the word. It involves understanding and aligning yourself with natural principles of science and learning to use these principles in a conscious and creative way. What this means from a practical standpoint is that we always attract into our lives what we think about the most, believe the most, and that to which we devote most of our emotional energy.

There are many examples in medicine, business, and sports where the condition of individuals and reaching outcomes are directly related to the constant and energetic process of visualizing their most desired expectations. I cannot overstate the importance of being specific and detailed in your visualization. The element of focused imagery and visualization is an integrated component of the formula that will truly supercharge your efforts and bring your most highly desired outcomes to successful and certain conclusions.

VISUALIZATION EXERCISE

1. Start with a movie of the future "you" that is richly compelling and attractive.

2. Then transport yourself next to that future successful "you." Observe your future self. Is this the person you desire and need to be? Make any adjustment in that person, (you) so that it will be. These can be conscious adjustments or you can adjust the image until it is fully attractive to you.

3. Next, step into that future "you", becoming him or her. Feel some of what that future "you" will feel. Enjoy it. Anticipate it. And now, look back from where you are in the future into that past where you were planning this goal and see the natural, inevitable path of steps that led up to now.

4. Then, step out of that future self and move back to the present, alongside your future timeline. Notice your future successes, your difficulties… and the resources you drew on to succeed.

5. Having come all the way back to the present, remember how you will inevitably get to that future, with enough of those feelings from the future to pull you forward and toward it.

6. Now, in the present, schedule your action plan. Put it on your calendar and in your schedule book. What will be the first thing you will do to let yourself know you are on the way to that goal?

Visualizing a New Reality

Creating a new reality is a matter of using the simple tools you have just learned. It doesn't need to be difficult or strained. It is easy and effortless when you allow yourself to imagine it and then place yourself in it, using all your senses.

Focus

FOCUS EXERCISE

Here's an exercise to get in touch with your senses. Schedule some time, at least 15 minutes, when you can be alone, quiet, and undisturbed.

Relax, get in touch with your breath.

ACTING FOR REAL

Dwell on what you need to be totally happy right now. If it is a 15 minute nap, take it!

FANTASY EXERCISE

Here is a fantasy in which your mind can create your ideal mini-vacation, giving you all the benefits without any of the problems. Create an imaginary world—see it, hear it, smell it, feel it, taste it.

My imaginary world is rich and prosperous beyond what I believe is possible on earth:

I have a family, just like my real family, only everyone is behaving exactly as I determine. I can even have a secret lover (but because my spouse is so wonderfully understanding, that doesn't even cross my mind!). My world has a beach with perfect waves, a cool pool with a waterfall flowing into it. A world of delight and pleasure and fun. And you should see how good I am at my favorite sport! How great my body looks and feels! In my imaginary land, there is no limit to fun, pleasure, and fulfillment. When I am tired of all this fun and pleasure, I take my leave to the real world, but I always bring a little of my imaginary world with me!

You can go to the most beautiful spots on the planet, but if you bring your "shoulds," your seriousness, and your stress consciousness with you, then you will not benefit.

Remember what you have read:

All significant and lasting change starts in the _____.

By modifying our _____ we modify our reality.

Start planning your future.

Things I need to change in my life:

Health:

Skills or Talents:

Money:

Work:

Leisure:

Relationships:

Spirituality:

Success:

The Roles We Play

Now it's time to get down to business! You have all the tools, so…
let's ACT NOW! Don't try—DO! Let's put everything we've
learned together to play your new empowered life character. Make
changes through playing roles. "All the world is a stage," so write
your life's screenplay, hire yourself as the director, and cast
yourself in the lead.

This is the realm of inventiveness and imagination. Play with
purpose and belief. A desire or purpose causes human action.

Acting for Real

Likewise, a desire or purpose causes dramatic action. The purpose comes from what a character needs to do or has to do within the given circumstances. Let your purpose come from within you!

CHAPTER 21
SURVIVAL INSTINCT

The obvious objective of all of the blueprints that we are given is simple survival. Most of us go through with one outcome, the one we are born with, which is our survival. I feel it's important for you to make the transition from *survival instincts* to *success intelligence* (discussed further in Chapter 24) by working and living smart. Don't just survive—succeed!

Sur·viv·al (n.)
1.   The state of remaining alive or in existence.

The word "survive" has become an overused and weighted word in our culture. Even more so recently, the word *survivor* has become a billion-dollar catchphrase. Look at the success of the reality show of the same name. The bottom line is, we're taking up a huge portion of our time trying to "survive." If you ask someone how he or she is doing, they'll frequently respond, "Oh, you know… surviving." Which essentially means that they believe that continuing to "not die" is sapping their energy and causing mental stress in their lives.

We are born with survival instincts. Our body has already been trained to do its very best to "not die" in every moment. Upon realizing that, we've expanded the term to include surviving our jobs, our relationships, and our daily stresses of life in the fast lane. And, of course, there is the all-important "paycheck to paycheck" survival. One must wonder where this concept of survival fits in Maslow's hierarchy of needs.

Perhaps the natural instinct of survival comes from the Stone Age, when our ancestors' daily stresses included avoiding being devoured by mastodons and dinosaurs on the way home from work. This instinct somehow carried through, and we still have a lesser strain of the instinct burning within us. However, with more rush hour road rage to deal with than large fanged mammals, we have applied survival to what we feel are our greatest stressors in the modern world.

The biggest and most popular of which is the almighty dollar. The "paycheck to paycheck" mentality drives us more than any other single force. Every mood we feel, every personal life decision that is made, and every perception of our lives that we have, seems to be based on whether or not we feel that we have enough resources (i.e. money).

Even the previously spiritual union of marriage has been infiltrated by money—the prenuptial agreement. We've become so convinced that bringing another person into our fragile financial ecosystem will disrupt the balance of our lives that we quickly make preparations for the financial disasters of a messy divorce—all before the flowers are even ordered! Weddings that used to begin with "We are gathered here in the presence of God to unite these two people…" will soon begin with "We are gathered here in the presence of the law firm of O'Malley, Rodriguez and Finklestein and the Bank of America to unite these two people…"

The perception of "not having enough" resources, has made life into an economic journey of "lack of." One facet of life (food, shelter, clothing, etc.) has single-handedly overshadowed all of the others and made itself into the factor that decides the quality of the others. How many times do we hear, "If only I had enough money for _____, then I would be happy"? We allow money (external) to determine our emotions (internal). That's like allowing the cart to lead the horse. The cart is a physical entity that has no more power than a dollar bill. It is only when we place emotional value on the piece of money that we give it the power to own our emotions, and therefore ourselves.

Therefore, to place the horse in front of the cart and allow your emotions to control your financial success, you must find the emotion that is to be the *chauffeur* that will drive *you* to success.

Fight or Flight

An extreme form of motivation that our body has in its blueprints is the fight-or-flight response. Most of you have probably heard about this in the context of the evening news: "Housewife lifts VW bug to save trapped baby!" No, this doesn't mean that prior to lifting her car the housewife was a superhero in disguise! In an emergency like this one, our bodies take the reins and *do what needs to be done.*

Do what needs to be done. This is an important concept because it proves that when we turn off our busy brains, we'll find that our bodies know what to do. I frequently tell my students, "Life is simple, but it's not easy!" Our bodies are already programmed with that information. We just tend to override it with our beliefs, neuroses, fears, and other things we do to fight the riptide. Well, the fight-or-flight response is one of our body's ways of reminding us of who's in charge.

Do you recall a time when you've been in danger, or feared that you could be in danger? Do you remember how the adrenaline pumped through your body, and how quickly you went into action? It's like turning your computer on. It's an automatic response. Whether you are in a dangerous situation or executing a danger situation, you hold your breath. When you are angry, scared, or startled you immediately pull air into your lungs and diaphragm and hold it there as a reservoir for your body to use and then release in small amounts until the danger situation is resolved.

For example, I was working with an inmate at a California prison on anger management and I taught him that all you have to do to control your anger is to breathe. You can't get mad, go mad, or be mad if you breathe.

Danger situations turn on your sensory acuity, which determines how you function using your five senses. At first, you stop breathing, and then your sensory acuity kicks in. Suddenly, your hearing, sight, smell, taste and everything you feel seems to be one hundred times bigger than before. The world is suddenly blown up to a thousand times its normal size and you are right in the eye of the storm. Your heart beats rapidly and then your breath becomes faster. This surge of adrenaline gives us the strength we need to either get the heck out of there, or stand our ground and fight off the danger. The fight-or-flight response is one of survival.

Now, the next time you see an actor in a movie or on television in a danger situation, you'll be able to observe them holding their breath right before the action starts. Try it and see how much fun it can be!

Here are some film examples in which the main character, like the housewife, was placed under threatening circumstances and was forced to become the unlikely hero: *Norma Rae*, *Fight Club*, *Superman*, *Spiderman*, *Air Force One*, and *Erin Brockovich*. Check out the actor's breathing patterns in the danger scenes and you'll see what I mean!

Emotional IQ

I spoke earlier about how an imbalance of emotions (such as jealousy) can throw you completely off balance. Along those lines, and also closely related to "work smart," is emotional IQ.

From the time we are children in school, the only type of IQ that seems to matter is, of course, the "all important" intellectual IQ. Recognizing strange patterns of shapes, endless word problems about trains and apples, and trying to relate strings of words to other strings of words, seems to somehow determine how far you will be able to go in life. Yet arguably more important is your emotional IQ. Sure the school IQ tests are great if you plan on sitting on a train platform for the rest of your life and predicting when train A and train B will collide. But what about *real* life? What happens when you go to an audition or job interview and you get the feeling that it's not going well, but don't know why? Or when you are suddenly in the middle of an argument with someone and don't remember how it started? What good are the trains and apples then?

No matter what you do for a living, your intelligence quotient (IQ) counts for, at most, 25% of your effectiveness. Your emotional intelligence (EQ), how well you deal with people, manage relationships, and understand yourself, counts for much of the rest. To reach the highest level of competence at work, you must know how to manage your emotions. You also must develop a fine sense of how other people feel—and what they need.

Neither emotional nor intellectual intelligence guarantees success. They are merely the raw materials needed to learn and develop the competence vital for top performance at work. For example, if you're in sales, empathy (tuning in to how others feel) must be translated into a set of concrete skills, such as listening to clients, seeing situations from their perspectives, and providing them with what they need. Your emotional intelligence depends on how well you master the "how to" below, which provides the foundation for the skills any job is likely to demand.

EMOTIONAL IQ EXERCISE

Look for emotional role models. If you know someone who is a wonderful listener, watch him or her closely. If not, try to visualize, in specific detail, just how such an expert would act. Pattern your own behavior after him using real, on-the-job situations as a learning lab.

How to Be Emotionally Intelligent

Be aware of your body. Posture and gesture reflect your feelings. For example, if your hands are clenched, what are you angry about?

Practice reading body signals. Turn down the sound on the television.

Notice which situations or people cause you problems. Work out why.

Anticipate situations you don't like. Think what you need to achieve and keep focused on it.

If you feel you're going to lose it, count to 10. Then ask, do I need to shout or do I have an alternative?

 Ask for feedback. Knowing how you come across identifies strengths and weaknesses.

Set achievable targets. For example, "I'm going to talk to two new people at the party," "I'm going to phone that new company and request a meeting to discuss opportunities."

Twice a day, listen to someone without interrupting. Then repeat what they say, "So you think…?" It helps you understand others' feelings.

ACTING FOR REAL

Image

The image you project will dictate the reactions of others towards you. The choice of how you cut your hair, dress, and groom is yours. However, if you dress below the expectations of others, you pay the price. The price is the service that you get, decreased credibility, and less income. Traditionally, those who dress up earn upper incomes. Through many surveys, tests and experience, I've totally convinced myself that people judge your worth, your background, your income, and your material worth by how you dress. Tom Peters, the renegade business guru, summed it up this way, "The bad guys win this one, dress for success."

Never assume that someone who dresses down is just as successful as they would be if they dressed up. Think of how much less effort they could have exerted in the process of achieving their position. Think of the possibility that they could have achieved even greater success through projecting an image in line with the expectations of those who are in decision-making positions.

So stop surviving and start succeeding! Begin with your attitude, be in BOP, nurture your emotional IQ, your EQ, by stopping, breathing, listening to others, and managing your emotions. Find a positive emotion to drive you to work smart. And while your eloquence will enhance your success, bear in mind that cultivating an image will boost your achievements even further.

CHAPTER 22
GOALS AND PLANS

Need vs. Want

If you're an actor, you must discover not the wants of the character, but the needs—and then heighten that. If a character is a drug addict and wants $100 to buy drugs, he will do nothing. If he needs the drugs, he will steal, kill, or do whatever it takes to get the drugs. A thief steals because of needs, not wants.

You won't get what you want unless you need it. If you are driven by your needs, you'll get what you want. Guaranteed.

"A career is a career, is a career…you just have to carve it out yourself."
                                                    —*Thom McFadden*

Getting What You Want

A happy, zestful life is, indeed, an attainable goal. It is the character we play. It is not what happens to us, but how we handle it, that determines our misery or well-being. Practically all man-made misery, or emotional turmoil and suffering, is the product of limited and distorted awareness—of erroneous values, concepts and assumptions, and of their ugly offspring, low self-esteem and the victim character (Chapter 19).

ACTING FOR REAL

Our adverse experiences, handicaps, and misfortunes are but the focus of our pain and unhappiness. The actual cause is how we perceive and react to them. It is our false or distorted perception and lack of understanding, our warped needs and wants, and the unwise means by which we attempt to achieve them that cause our self-rejection and hurting. We can successfully deal only with what is—not with what we wish or want when this is contrary to reality.

I find the fundamental block to personal happiness and harmonious, loving relationships to be a lack of awareness of the factors that influence our individual behavior. I am confident that you will conclude, as I believe, that all antisocial and harmful acts are the result of one's limited and distorted awareness and his resulting self-rejection and hurting. He is playing the wrong part.

BOP, or awareness—as we use a mere fraction of the term—is the degree of clarity with which we perceive and understand, both consciously and unconsciously, all factors that affect our lives. Next to life and death, being in BOP is the most vital factor in our human existence. It determines our needs and how we fulfill them, how we feel towards ourselves—i.e., our self-esteem—and how we relate to our family and fellow men and women. In fact, our individual degree of awareness is the only limiting factor as to how wisely and harmoniously we act and react, both at work and "at play." Thus, it actually determines our degree of well-being, happiness, and zest for living. It is responsible for every choice and decision we make! It determines the characters we play, our dark characters, or our enlightened Acting for Real characters.

Inadequate self-esteem is basically a problem in awareness, or not being in BOP. It results from a mind that has been programmed (i.e., conditioned) by false and distorted concepts and has thus developed a lifestyle that perpetuates and augments one's feelings of inadequacy, futility, and sense of personal unworthiness. Adherence to distorted values generates a desperate and compulsive need to be "better than," a compulsion that is the root of our personal and social problems.

Why vs. How

People are interested in why things happen. They consult psychotherapists, psychics, and anyone else who might be able to figure out why their lives have turned out the way they have. Why their childhood was the way it was, why their parents did what they did to them, and why they act the way they do.

"Why" is in the past. Acting for Real centers not on the why, but on the "how." How to take action! How to duplicate behaviors that work, how to play the characters that will empower you, and how to nuke the characters and behaviors that don't work. If you understand the "how," you have the power to duplicate, negate, or kill the behavior or action that is leading to an outcome.

All the positive beliefs, great attitudes, and empowered characters in the world won't drive you to success, unless you have a concrete set of goals in mind to work toward. Let's set those goals and, using our enlightened life characters, power toward reaching them!

Dreams Into Goals

A goal is a dream with a date attached.

Goals need to be **SMART**:

1. **S** aid
2. **M** otivated
3. **A** cted
4. **R** ealistic
5. **T** imed

The greatest danger of all for most of us, is not that our aim is too high and we miss it, but that we aim too low and we reach it.

♦ Goals give us purpose for our actions.

♦ Goals help to motivate.

♦ Goals help you achieve a daily routine.

♦ Goals help you control & manage time more efficiently.

♦ Goals help you track your progress.

♦ Goals build your confidence as you succeed.

♦ Goals help you achieve success.

♦ Goals will increase your income.

♦ Goals give direction.

Many a study has been done on successful individuals who all make lists and set goals. Your goals should be achieved through vision, planning, and time management. Set your own goals, write them down, and walk to the beat of your own drum. Do not be afraid to take calculated risks. See yourself seizing opportunities and reaping the rewards. The person who sees opportunities and is willing to work hard is the person who will be "lucky" in the end. There is no such thing as luck, only outcomes. The harder you work on your goals, the more positive outcomes you will have. It's that simple.

Either you set your own goals, or someone else will set them for

you—making you their slave!

Goal Setting

If you desire success and happiness in your life, you must first establish a definite goal for yourself. You must plan and strive. Very few people clearly understand the difference between vague hopes and wishes and a defined, focused goal. This is why so few people ever attain what they thought were goals. Effective and constant communication with yourself is essential.

Write down your outcomes and plan your daily activities that are needed to accomplish them—your daily outcomes. You must develop a list of things you are driven to accomplish in your lifetime, one day at a time. Let your values, beliefs, and dreams come into play. Having a strong purpose behind your daily activities—knowing why you are taking action—will give you the strength to persevere. Let your goals inspire you to make plans and develop a strategy to succeed. Success and happiness is something you definitely need to pay for in advance.

In setting your goals, you should give careful thought to one major goal that is supported by several secondary goals. These secondary goals should be supported by action plans. What are you willing to give up in order to achieve your goals? Watching less TV would be a good start for most people. Take responsibility for your happiness and increase your self-discipline. You are it; there is no one else to depend on to do it for you. Break your action plans down into yearly, quarterly, monthly and daily activities to set a workable plan and timeline for your achievements. Review your goals and plans daily to keep yourself on course. Adjustments in your goals, plans, or strategies may be needed from time to time as changes occur in your life. With your goals clearly stated and a plan of action organized and implemented, you will be more in control of your life and obtain more inner peace.

Keep in mind that it all begins with a great attitude! As we've discussed, our attitude has a profound impact on the quality of our lives. It can make or break you. Your reactions to events that happen in your life are far more important than the actual events. You cannot change the past or predict the future and you cannot control happenstance. Challenges will continue to occur in your life. The only thing over which you have complete control each and every day is your attitude. Your attitude about yourself is the perfect place to start. Each of us is born with unlimited potential. Your self-esteem is a function of the continuity between your beliefs, values, and your actions. Act with integrity, creativity, and style.

Create balance in your life. Too much of anything is not healthy. Your lifestyle plan should include moving in a positive direction mentally, physically, and spiritually. Be BOP! Positive actions become habits with consistent repetition. Strive to master yourself, your emotions, and your mindset. Form good habits and become their servant.

Put at least one hour aside each day to study. Always continue to learn. Exercise and eat properly to help produce the energy needed to take action. Delay temporary gratification for long-term success. Don't procrastinate, just do it. Create a sense of urgency. Organize your personal and professional life. Once you're rolling, seek to increase the rate of your accomplishments.

Surround yourself with positive, optimistic people because it creates the atmosphere you need to achieve. You will get what you desire by helping others get what they need. Effective communication with others is critical. Love and respect yourself and others every day. Teamwork and cooperation is essential. Encourage creativity within boundaries. Encourage others to adopt a be BOP attitude. Try not to condemn, complain, or criticize. Find out what interests others. Express appreciation for others and make them feel important. Be sincere and enthusiastic. Always be honest and true. Make the most of your talents and abilities. Continue developing and striving for excellence. Gain a reputation of good character. Give from your heart and it will always come back to you tenfold.

Time is your most precious commodity. How you positively and constructively budget your time will have a great impact on your success. A daily calendar is a must. There are daily planners and organizers available that are developed specifically for your business.

Life can, at times, get a bit overwhelming. When it does, it's okay to take a break and rest, but never quit. Go punch a pillow, scream, cry, pray, meditate or talk with someone who cares. Get out and have fun! Do charity work. After you rebound, get back to it. Almost all successful and happy people have experienced many painful failures. Use your faith to embrace and transform suffering by accepting its purifying value. Do not let it defeat you. Persist. Be courageous. Be determined. Always maintain a sense of humor. Take time to laugh and smile. Validate yourself! Foster your enlightened triangle.

COMMITMENT

"Thom takes a wife." Thom and Nancy's wedding
invitation drawn by artist Billy Bloomfield

ACTING FOR REAL

Commitment

"Until one is committed, there is hesitancy, the chance to draw back-—Concerning all acts of initiative (and creation), there is one elementary truth that ignorance of which kills countless ideas and splendid plans: that the moment one definitely commits oneself, then Providence moves too. All sorts of things occur to help one that would never otherwise have occurred. A whole stream of events issues from the decision, raising in one's favor all manner of unforeseen incidents and meetings and material assistance, which no man could have dreamed would have come his way. Whatever you can do, or dream you can do, begin it. Boldness has genius, power, and magic in it. Begin it now."

Johann Wolfgang von Goethe

Today more than ever, our focus needs to be committing to our goals. A person without a goal is a person without direction. However, merely setting a goal is not sufficient if one needs to achieve greater gains than those of the past. You must make that all-important mental connection to your goal as commitment. That is when you make a conscious decision that regardless of how many roadblocks or detours you encounter as you move toward your goal, you will keep on keeping on. The goal must be reached. If your goal is a big one, you are going to encounter problems and you will have to be strong to overcome them. Every project has within it an escape hatch, and if you are not committed to getting the job done, you will hit the escape hatch and never realize what you were capable of doing. If someone is not committed to a goal and hits the escape hatch, they end up settling for failure. Yet rarely do they blame themselves. The saddest thing about quitting is that every time someone quits, it becomes a little easier to do the same thing the next time the going gets tough. The beautiful part of being committed to your goal is that every time you press on and go over the hurdle, it becomes easier for you to handle the next problem when it comes along. You eventually form the habit of winning. Make a binding commitment to your goal. It will virtually blind you from many of the small annoyances that would otherwise distract and confuse you.

ACTING FOR REAL

Commitment checklist:

✓ Belief and conviction in the value and service you provide.

✓ Clearly identify your goals, see them, hear them, feel them, and taste them.

✓ Internalize the rational reasons why you need to achieve your goals.

✓ Clearly see the steps required and make your plan of action.

✓ Identify the key result areas.

✓ Break activities into bite-size pieces.

✓ Confirm it is physically possible to achieve the goals.

✓ Maintain your focus on your goals, not on the obstacles.

✓ See yourself successfully achieving your goals and enjoying the rewards.

✓ Confirm that you are willing to do whatever it takes to have those rewards.

✓ Focus on the rewards, not the pain and pitfalls.

✓ Make commitments to others who will help to hold you accountable.

✓ Always be the best you can possibly be.

✓ Give yourself reward incentives.

✓ Challenge yourself to break old, conditioned habits.

✓ Chart your progress on a calendar.

✓ Risk and stretch yourself. Understand that we grow when we challenge ourselves and bust out of our comfort zones.

✓ Make a firm and binding contract with yourself.

Commitment is what transforms a promise into reality. It is the energy, the electrical current that makes things happen. Commitment is the power that changes the very face of reality. Commitment is no idle thought; it is the sailor thrown into the waters of the turbulent sea with no place to swim except to shore. It's then death in the deep sea, or swim for shore. There is no acceptable choice except for the sailor to head for the shore. That's when commitment comes in, through hell or high water, nothing stands in the way. There is no force on earth like that of someone who is committed. When it's death or shore, that, my friend, is when someone is "committed."

Commitment is not easy. It is making the time when there is none. It is overcoming what appears to be impossible. It is overcoming what appears to be insurmountable obstacles. It is the daily triumph of belief over skepticism. It is hanging in there through failure after failure, through hardships and obstacles, coming through time after time, day after day, week after week, month after month, and year after year.

Commitment is more than just wanting to do something and saying, "If I have the time, if the right circumstances occur, or if someone else starts off the process." It is about choosing to be effective and about saying "I will." It's not about trying, because trying is the prerequisite for failure.

It is about being out there, exposed and vulnerable, maybe even subject to ridicule because in this world, intensity is considered bad form. Commitment has its rewards. It is feeling good about yourself because you know you are being true to yourself and your word. It is what brings a light to our faces and our lives.

As George Bernard Shaw said:

I am of the opinion that my life belongs to the whole community, and as long as I live, it is my privilege to do for it whatever I can. I want to be thoroughly used up when I die, for the harder I work, the more I live. I rejoice in life for its own sake. Life is not a brief candle to me. It is sort of a splendid torch which I have got hold of for the moment, and I want to make it burn as brightly as possible before handing it on to future generations.

Commitment is doing whatever it takes!

Discipline

"Discipline is the refining fire by which talent becomes ability."
—Roy L. Smith

THE FIRST STEP IS THE HARDEST.

If you can get up the courage to begin, you have the courage to succeed. Begin where you are, work where you are. The hour that you are now wasting, dreaming of some far-off success, is crowded with grand possibilities.

The first essential of success is that you begin. Once you have started, all that is within and without you will come to your assistance. Do not wait. The time will never be "just right." Start where you stand and work with whatever tools you have at your command. Better tools will be found as you go along. Eighty percent of success is showing up.

If you desire to rise above average in any endeavor, you have to be willing to be disciplined. Albert Gray said, "The common denominator of success lies in forming the habit of doing things that failures don't like to do." All the talent in the world won't matter in the long run if you can't manage it properly in the short run.

Just Do It

Actually sit down and take the time to do it. If this made the difference between success and failure, you would do it, wouldn't you? Well, it does make the difference, so do it!

BE REALISTIC
Don't set fantasy goals. If your goal is to have a six-figure income, don't expect that in six months. It could take one to three years to achieve.

GOALS MUST BE MEASURABLE
Break goals down into small steps. Set daily goals, start-up goals (one to three months), short term (one year), medium range (one to three years), and long range (three to five years).

ACTING FOR REAL

BE SPECIFIC

Be specific, not general, in describing your goals. Instead of, "I want to own a house," describe the house in detail: price range, what you need financially to make it happen, and the date that you would like to own it.

BE REALISTIC WITH TIME

Determine what actions are needed to accomplish each goal and a realistic time frame in which to achieve them.

CHALLENGE YOURSELF

Make your goals interesting and worth stretching yourself for. Get out of your comfort zone and enjoy the challenge.

BE FLEXIBLE

If you don't make the goal you set, don't get down on yourself. Reevaluate the time frame and go for it again. Be persistent.

GOALS SHOULD BE WRITTEN:

Record goals on paper, otherwise they are only dreams.

And finally…

"Funny is money"

"Simplicity is paramount in comedy"

"Seeing is believing"

You're motivated, inspired, aware, working smart, thinking smart, committed, disciplined and ready to grab the brass ring! Now what? Construct your determination with sustained effort, controlled attention, and concentrated energy. Opportunities never come to those who wait. They are captured by those who dare to act!

Most people have had little or no success in achieving goals they have set for themselves. People are tired of the pain and guilt associated with breaking New Year's Resolutions and their unfulfilled goals. They find it easier to ignore them. People will go through the motions of setting goals if someone presses them to do the "drill." As they are "setting" their goals, they already expect failure.

A wise man once said, "He who has limp vision remains impotent forever." People constantly set goals with limp vision and impotent results. The weight loss industry provides an excellent example. At any one time, 70-percent of the adult population is on some kind of diet. The other 30-percent probably just finished a diet or are planning to go on one. People approach these diets by looking for a quick fix. They are not prepared for the required lifestyle change that diet success demands. As a result, these new "30-day wonder diets" provide weight loss for a month and that is mostly water loss.

We know that moving toward pleasure and away from pain dictates our behavior. Our subconscious is 25 times more powerful than our conscious mind's willpower in controlling our behavior. So, if our subconscious associates more pain than pleasure with dieting, what do you think the results will be? Your subconscious mind is the seat of memory, imagination, and creativity and controls all major body systems. However, the subconscious has a mental age equal to a bright 5 to 7-year-old. How's this for a scenario? Your subconscious stores all emotions, both pleasant and unpleasant and all experiences, both pleasant and unpleasant. Now, assuming that, like most people, your dieting experience has resulted in general dissatisfaction, self-denial, discouragement, anxiety, and feelings of guilt, what will your subconscious "think" when you say, "I'm going on a diet"?

I'll tell you what it thinks. Let's spell out in big, bold letters, the word "DIET." Now let's underline the first three letters, <u>DIE</u>T and that is what the subconscious thinks! Now you tell me, given the power and emotional control that the subconscious has, how easy will the subconscious make your dieting effort? If you are serious about changing your weight, avoid using the word "diet." Your prior experience with that word has been too negative. Replace that word with "weight management."

Now, let's return to a word, that most people find equally negative and unfulfilling, the word "goals". People have failed at achieving goals the same way they have failed in their string of diet programs. A study conducted at Yale University demonstrates the correlation between clearly stated written objectives, and performance.

The 1953 graduating class at Yale University was the target group for this study. At graduation, class members were asked if they had a clear set of objectives written down and a plan for achieving those objectives. Listen to this! Only three percent of this prestigious, success-oriented, Ivy League class reported they had written goals. Twenty years later, in 1973, the surviving members of that graduating class were interviewed. The study discovered that the three percent of graduates who had specific and written objectives when they left Yale were, as a group, more financially successful than the other 97-percent of this class combined!

Eighty-five percent of your success will be determined by how you answer the question, "Why do you need to achieve "X"? You, of course, will define "X." Your answers to this "why" question will be given with emotionally based words. And emotions literally propel us to our objective; they are our chauffeurs to success. If our emotions are weak and unfocused, our results will be negligible. If there is great passion behind our "why?" and provided we are also clearly focused, our lives can literally be transformed overnight.

ACTING FOR REAL

Personal Success Plan

I. *Crystallize your thinking.*

    Determine what specific outcome you need to achieve.
    Then dedicate yourself to its attainment with
    unswerving singleness of purpose, the trenchant zeal of
    a crusader. Be possessed.

II. *Develop a plan for achieving your outcome, and a*
    deadline for its attainment.

    Plan your progress carefully. Organized activity and
    maintained enthusiasm are the wellsprings of your
    power.

III. *Develop a sincere desire for the things you need in your*
    life.

    A burning desire is the greatest motivator of every
    human action. The desire for success implants "success
    consciousness" which, in turn, creates a vigorous and
    ever-increasing "habit of success."

IV. *Develop supreme confidence in yourself and your own*
    abilities.

    Enter every activity without giving mental recognition
    to the possibility of defeat. Concentrate on your

strengths, instead of your weaknesses… on your powers, instead of your problems.

V.   *Develop a dogged determination to follow through on your plan, regardless of obstacles, criticism, or circumstances, or what other people say, think, or do!*

Thom and Nancy at their ranch-style wedding in Malibu
with Marcia and Neil Diamond

CHAPTER 23
REHEARSAL: PERFECT PRACTICE

"The road to success is dotted with many tempting parking places."

—Anonymous

Motivation

There are no failures, only outcomes. We all know someone who has taken the leap into some sort of business venture or project with the aim of success. More often than not, you'll hear about their "backup plans," "safety net," and phrases like, "I'm just being realistic." Despite these apparently wise intentions, each of these phrases indicates an expectation of a negative outcome. Just like trying is a prerequisite for failure.

mo·ti·va·tion (n.)
1. The act of giving somebody a reason or incentive to do something.
2. A reason for doing something or behaving in some way.

To take action requires motivation! To be motivated is to need to do a specific thing more than we need to do anything else at that particular time. Even though we may not be aware of the specific desire, motivation is what we most need to do, in the sense of what we would rather do than not do. There are many things to motivate us. Probably the greatest handicap to understanding motivation is our conditioned concept that we are motivated to do only what we find pleasure in doing. Such is not the case.

ACTING FOR REAL

Let us look beyond motivation. When we do so, it is apparent that every human act is a response to a personal need or desire. Our basic need is to be comfortable—physically, mentally, and emotionally. Thus, our fundamental motivations, in a total sense, are to "feel good," or at least to feel as good as the given circumstances allow.

To go a step further, it is also apparent that our unfulfilled needs generate tensions. Thus, to "feel good," i.e., to be comfortable, we must resolve or satisfy these tensions. Such tensions may be generated by fear, cold, pain, hunger for food, sex, our need for attention, to win, to succeed, our need for confirmation and agreement, for acceptance and approval, to be liked or loved, our fear of what others may think or say, or any type of force or coercion. For example, I may have a strong value against bearing arms and killing my fellow men. If, however, I am faced with the alternative of going to prison, or possibly getting shot, I might well be motivated to bear arms. The deciding point would be my willingness or unwillingness to pay the price demanded for not going to war.

Unless I perceive how I can benefit my particular need by the proposed act or endeavor, I will continue with what I am currently doing. For instance, for me to get up out of bed in the morning, I must perceive that by so doing I am fulfilling a personal need. Such need may be to get some food in my stomach, to meet my personal commitment to be active and productive, to keep from losing my job, or simply to maintain the approval of my neighbors.

I normally, of course, operate under several nonconflicting motivations at any given time, such as a desire to achieve material success, improve my golf game, or make my spouse happy.

In the final analysis, motivation is simply a matter of perceiving that the potential benefits of a given action outweigh the price demanded, and that is the most desirable alternative available for meeting the need in question. Only the relevant factors of our prevailing awareness can determine the accuracy of our perception and how wise or unwise the resulting action. Most personal confusion and conflict stem from not clarifying our motivation, from not making a total decision to pay or not to pay the price demanded for our competing desires.

To change our motivation, we must become aware, whether of a greater need or of a more beneficial means of fulfilling our existing need. Such change in our awareness may come about through our own or others' efforts, or simply the force of circumstances. It is essential, however, that if the change is to come through our own conscious efforts that we ourselves have the awareness to be motivated to make such efforts. To say one should or should not do a certain thing is, therefore, quite meaningless if the individual does not have the awareness to be so motivated.

ACTING FOR REAL

Sewing the Safety Net

The "magic if" places you into the future that you create for yourself. You place yourself in the future of your choosing. When taking action towards your goals, stopping to ask questions such as, "What if my outcome is negative?" places you in that negative outcome. In that situation, your *action* is the negative outcome. By saying "What if I succeed?" or better, "I will succeed," you are placing yourself in a future where the action is success!

If you were a tightrope walker, you would know the importance of a good, sturdy net below you. But what if you became so nervous about walking the rope that you ended up spending all your time below, carefully sewing and reinforcing the net? After some time, you might end up spending so much time sewing the net that you would eventually lose the courage to climb the ladder and actually walk the tightrope.

Now use your powers of visualization and place yourself in the circus tent under that tightrope. It is opening night and a rainbow of floodlights sweep over the other performers and the eager crowd. Smell the smells, hear the sounds of the big top around you, feel the cool tarp under your feet and the powder that you work through your fingers. As you stand at the foot of the ladder, the net hangs just over your head and the tightrope seems to be hanging from the stars that peek through the top of the tent. You start to sweat, you can feel your heart pounding in your chest and you become conscious of your breath speeding up. Don't panic—this is normal. It's called the fight-or-flight response and it is putting you to the test—your moment of truth. Are you going to run out of the tent to the safety of your car, parked snugly in a primo spot with a six pack of beer with your name on it waiting for you? Or are you going to suck it up and climb up the ladder?

You decide to go for it and shakily start the climb up to the tightrope. At first your legs are shaking so badly that you think they will collapse under you and you will fall backwards to the ground with a crashing thud. You wince at the thought of it and tighten your grip on the rungs as you climb higher and higher above the murmuring crowd below. You are suddenly level with the net, and then it too drops further and further below you until it becomes as small as the crowd. Sweat seems to be pouring off you and the powder on your hands is turning to glue. *Lub-dub, lub-dub...* Your heart and lungs plead with you to go back down the ladder. Your brain and inner critic remind you of how nice that first sip of beer would taste in the plush bucket seat of your car with some Jimmy Buffett to serenade you. But you are possessed and continue on. You must get across that tightrope. You are petrified but have decided that nothing will stop you.

Once at the top, you grasp the pole that will keep you balanced as you cross the rope. At the same time, you realize that you will ultimately be the one to keep yourself balanced. You have everything it takes to do this. You have been working toward this for a long time, your tools are sharpened and ready to go, you are balanced, and your senses are functioning perfectly. You see the rope in front of you, hear your bare feet as they fall gently onto the rope in each perfectly timed step, and feel the rope in the perfect center of your foot. Be BOP!

Before you know it, you have successfully crossed the tightrope and you grandly acknowledge the roaring applause of the crowd below! You knew ahead of time that you could do it, didn't consider the option of not doing it or failing, and you did it. Try applying such a visualization to one of your goals. Walk yourself down the path to achieving one of your goals from beginning to end. *Perfect practice makes perfect.* By visualizing how you will succeed, you are allowing your subconscious to actually practice the process of succeeding. Therefore, when you actually, physically start working toward achieving your goal, your subconscious will believe that *you have already done it before*—perfectly. And that you can do it again! Plant the seeds that give you the confidence you need to succeed.

Covering your bases when starting out on your road to success is one thing. But once you have an adequate "Plan B"—the absolute least amount of "negative" planning that you can do—it should only cover extreme emergencies (lack of food, shelter, clothing). Anything more is counterproductive to everything else you are doing to be successful! Don't fight against your own forward motion before you even start moving. Give yourself every chance at success—you deserve it!

By developing and committing to this mode of thinking, you are creating a positive character. This is the character that is also known as your chauffeur to success. This is the entity that *you will become* whenever you decide to go after something that you must have—a dream, a goal, or a future. Developing positive characters will empower you. Developing negative characters will set you up for negative outcomes every time. Action!

Paths to Positive Thinking

1. Work on making yourself happy before trying to please others. Smile and the world smiles with you.

2. Program yourself to be positive.

3. Rise above your ego (the need to be right).

4. Look for contradictory evidence whenever you see something you don't like in someone.

5. Stop seeing the differences in people and appreciate the similarities.

6. Be true to yourself.

7. Do the best you can and appreciate that you did.

8. Walk the walk of enthusiasm, talk the talk of enthusiasm, feel the power of enthusiasm, and you will reap the rewards of enthusiasm.

9. Start everyday with creativity. This forces you to be positive. To be creative uses the right side of your brain for the right results.

10. Look for ways to help others.

11. Do not participate in complaining sessions.

12. Look for the good in others.

13. Don't criticize, condemn, or complain.

14. Justify the behavior of others by where they are in their path to a higher level of awareness.

15. Become genuinely interested in other people.

16. Remember that a person's name is music to their ears.

17. Be a good listener. Encourage others to talk about themselves.

18. Cooperate with the inevitable.

19. Expect ingratitude and do not expect rewards.

20. Model the best to be the best.

21. Follow your spiritual beliefs.

Taking Action

So there it is in a nutshell. If you desire to supercharge your success and propel yourself forward at warp speed, don't reinvent the wheel and don't waste time with theoreticians whose success is not worth emulating. Remember, the world is full of do-gooders who are long on advice but short on wisdom.

Seek out the very best models you can find in your fields of interest and observe them with unrelenting passion. Observation is one of the simplest and easiest ways to dramatically shrink the amount of time it will take you to accomplish your intended future. Observation is the secret weapon of the master modeler. Start adding this weapon to your arsenal today.

The reason modeling is such a vital learning tool is that it forces you to discard all the theoretical fluff, the unproven ideas and opinions, and zero in on techniques that have been successfully implemented. Remember, to become the best, observe people who have already succeeded, people who are already the "best."

Suppose you own a business. You need to learn how to improve the impression your customers have of you and your company. Where would you turn for the answer? To instincts, classes, seminars, manuals, texts, or intuition? If you are one of the masses, these are the places you turn. However, by following the models put forth in this book, you will find the practical knowledge and experience necessary for success. You will add to your chances for success by being in BOP, balanced, observant, and in present time.

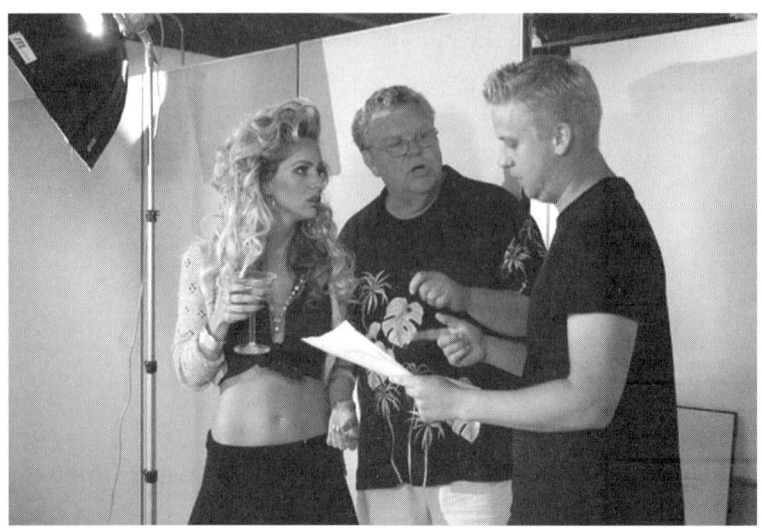

Actress Julia Galasso with Thom and son, director/
producer James McFadden, on the set of GoPotato.tv's
Sweet Dreams series

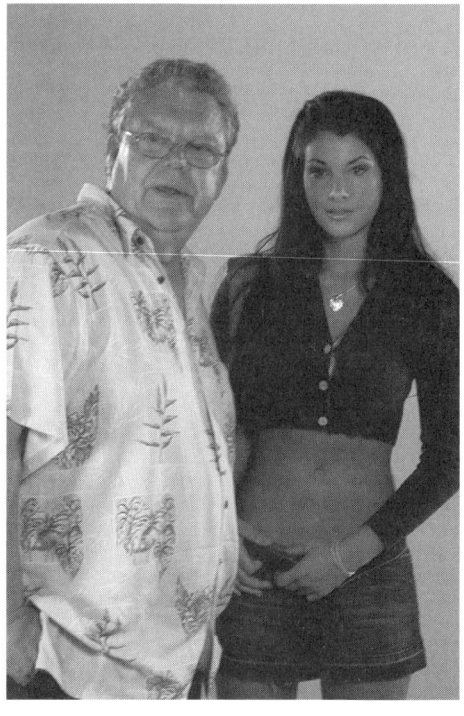

Thom with actress Cora Skinner on the set of *Sweet Dreams*

CHAPTER 24
SURVIVAL TO SUCCESS

Our Basic Need

Our basic need and urge is to "feel good" about ourselves, mentally, physically and emotionally—to heighten the life of our "I AM" personality. This need is responsible for our ultimate motivation. Regardless of our immediate objective, everything we do is to achieve a sense of total well-being. Unfortunately, a few, if indeed any of us, have sufficient awareness to always know what will make us feel really good about ourselves. Herein lies our crucial need for good self-esteem, for we cannot possibly feel good and be at peace with ourselves without a significant sense of adequacy and self-worth.

All of our goals, hopes, and aspirations are based on this fundamental need. The more limited and distorted our awareness, the more misleading and unfulfilling are our efforts. For example, we drink, we smoke, we take drugs, and we pursue and worship sex in all its phases as if it were some kind of god. We have compulsive needs to win, to be "better than," to avoid mistakes, to help others, to straighten people out, to accumulate wealth we can never use, to gain power and prestige, to eat all the rich, expensive foods we can stuff into our mouths, or whatever. We have a desperate urge to love and to be loved, to be accepted and approved, to be respected and looked up to, on and on, *ad infinitum.* Our ultimate motivation is our universal need to "feel good."

Thus, the only true measure of success is the degree to which one actually does "feel good" about oneself, despite one's particular degree of material prosperity or prestige. Our only limitation to achieving this ultimate objective is our limited and distorted awareness. We are not in BOP!

The test, of course, is our peace of mind and overall sense of well-being. This art is what self-esteem is all about, for whether or not we realize it, practically our every endeavor is an indirect attempt to gain a sense of self-worth so that we can approve and "feel good" towards ourselves. Once we are able to feel good about ourselves, we are able to move out of survival mode and into success mode.

Success Intelligence

"If you cater to the masses you can dine with the classes."
                                                        —Unknown

SURVIVAL INSTINCTS   →   SUCCESS INTELLIGENCE

Success intelligence is simply this: get smart, think smart, be smart, work smart. In other words, if you're not thinking smart, get smart! If you're not being smart, think smart! If you're not working smart, be smart! If you're not getting smart, work smart! As you can see, success intelligence is mining our minds. If you think a situation is going wrong, or your plans are not going according to plan, make adjustments. Don't delay to the point where you find yourself completely off course. It's just like sailing. If a 65-degree course is going to take you straight home, the shortest distance, and you sail one degree off course, you will find that the longer you wait to make the adjustment, the further away you will be from your destination. One degree off course can add hours, even days, to your travels. Thus is life. Don't be afraid to make changes just because it will mean going backwards for a minute. Remember, it was that minute that got you off course in the first place. Take a minute to think smart about it!

Success intelligence is about finding a smart path, a path that will most quickly and assuredly lead you to success. A tried and true path to success in the professional world is to find a need and fill it. Find a product or service that appeals to the most people possible. Here is a famous example of that philosophy at work. Steve Jobs co-founded Apple Computers in 1976 and Pixar, the Academy-Award-winning computer animation studios, in 1986. Apple continues to be a leader in personal computing devices that cater to students, educators, creative professionals, and consumers around the world. Pixar has created half of the top six domestic grossing animated films of all time, including *Toy Story* (1995), *A Bug's Life* (1998), *Toy Story 2* (1999), and *Monsters, Inc.* (2001). Each film was released under Pixar's partnership with Walt Disney Pictures and became the highest grossing animated film for the year it was released.

ACTING FOR REAL

This is a man who saw a need in society, created a way to fill that need, and did it in a way that appealed to everyone from children to CEOs of the largest companies in the world.

You cannot drive yourself to success—you have to be driven!

Your Chauffeurs to Success

e·mo·tion (n.)

1. A strong feeling; excitement; a state of consciousness having to do with the arousal of feelings, distinguished from other mental states, as cognition, volition, and awareness of physical sensation.

And finally, we reach the real secret to your success in the universe—your chauffeur to success. You cannot drive yourself to success. You must develop an emotion or emotions that drive you to success. Imagine that you can be a passenger in any car you desire.

In the universe, you *are* that passenger and you *have* that choice. As for the driver, I have found six different sources of power that people most often use to "drive themselves to success." I call these the Six Dominant Emotions. As you'll find, some are more powerful than others, and none work unless they are used in moderation and balanced with the others.

The Six Dominant Emotions that drive you to success:

1. Greed

2. Fear of Poverty

3. Pride

4. Love of Work

5. Love of People

6. Love of Spirituality

The Dark Triad

The first three emotions are what I call the "Dark Triad." These sentiments come naturally to us as impulses. We are naturally attracted to feeling them and, if left unchecked, they can carry us away like a stream into a waterfall. They are the easiest to fall into and the most difficult to get out of. While this triad will certainly affect our drive to success, they should definitely not be in the driver's seat. In other words, they should not be our chauffeurs to success. The three emotions of the Dark Triad are described as follows: greed, fear of poverty, and pride.

ACTING FOR REAL

Greed

Let us imagine what our ride would be like with greed as our chauffeur. Our vehicle would be armored with several security systems to keep out unwanted riders and guests. Anyone wanting to ride with us would have to pay a significant fee for the use of our time, energy, and resources. Other drivers would have to wait behind us for gasoline, car washes, and repairs because our needs would, of course, come first. Others would be forced to pull over and yield to us because our vehicle would always have the right of way.

Greed, or lust for power, is the driving force behind many apparently successful people. Usually, as in the cases of Napoleon, Hitler, and Mussolini, they overreach themselves and end in failure. The history of these tyrants does show, however, that a powerful emotion, even a *questionable* one, often leads to efficiency and temporary success.

But there is in all of us what cynics call the herd instincts, what psychologists call the social instincts and what theologians call conscience. They inspire such feelings as pity, generosity, loyalty, patriotism, love, charity, tolerance, and appreciation. They are deeply rooted, because nature knows that, without them, people cannot live together and survive.

These feelings clash with greed, or lust for power, the conflict leading to indecision, worry, fear, procrastination, laziness or escape into nonproductive activity. Not many people are so deficient in the social instincts that they can successfully make greed, or lust for power, their dominant motive. Hitler and Mussolini became insane, and I doubt whether modern psychiatrists would consider Napoleon sane.

Do you think you could keep your balance if you deliberately cultivated greed or lust for power? The very distaste with which you contemplate the idea shows that emotional conflict and inefficiency would result. Only people already unbalanced can power their success with such a driving force. If you are playing the part of Power in your Creative Triangle, how can you balance it? Look at the Creative Wheel of Behavior and steady your out-of-balance personality by looking to its opposition. You will notice that across the wheel from the Power/ Paranoia personality is the Humanities/ Passion personality—the enlightened and therefore, more triumphant personality. What is the part you are playing in your triangle? Are you playing any of the parts from the dark side of the wheel? If so, look to its opposition in the Creative Wheel of Behavior to find a more straightforward path.

Fear of Poverty

Now we are driven with the fear of poverty as a chauffeur. The car is small and held together by old rusty parts because we are too cheap to have a nice car or even splurge for decent parts for this old hunk of junk. The driver is unwilling to even put gasoline or oil in the car so we are basically running on fumes at this point. We may take pride in being thrifty, but we unknowingly passed thrifty about 70 miles ago and stupidly kept on going! Now we have strayed so far off the path to our dreams that we were on that we can hardly remember how we ended up here. Even common sense can turn on you if you let it become the central driving force (chauffeur) of your life. An abundance of anything—including fear—will throw you off balance and out of BOP.

Fear of poverty is, therefore, not recommended, though undoubtedly it is the driving force behind many moderately successful people. It leads many people to learn a trade or profession and to work reasonably hard at their jobs.

But intense fear cannot be long-sustained in the normal mind. It can inspire a short burst of effort, but generally not much more. Where, in abnormal cases, the fear is sustained and becomes a dominant emotion, it has a paralyzing effect if not a disastrous one. Even a mild fear of poverty will cause worry, the postponing of decisions, unwillingness to try anything new, reluctance to make changes and dissatisfaction with routine.

Mistakes of the past, the chances lost, together with the probable mistakes of the present and future, preoccupy the mind until the victim is hardly capable of decisive, courageous action or long-sustained purpose. Nature designed fear as a useful emotion only in rare emergencies, when extreme danger makes a sudden burst of speed. It is quite a useful emotion when you are chased by a bull or must quickly dodge a speeding automobile.

In these types of situations, it is associated with the fight-or-flight response, which is essentially a panic attack. During such times, a person will forget to breathe, their heart will race, and their ability to think will come to a halt, being replaced instead by pure adrenaline. Therefore, the chances of achieving any kind of quality, lasting success in a state of fear are slim to none. Even if it were possible, one would simply not be able to sustain such a physical state for any period of time without exhaustion and eventually death. Nobody has ever achieved substantial success through fear of poverty (or any other fear for that matter).

Another name for fear of poverty is desire for security. It is the same old fear in milder form, and no *mild* emotion can become your center of power. Only a strong emotion can drive you to success. The failure of most people is that this rather sickly emotion, the desire for security, is their chief motive for working. They are fortunate that conflicting emotions gain the upper hand most of the time, thus preventing it from becoming an obsessing fear of poverty with all its associated evils.

Many people think they deserve credit because their ambitions are small and their main desire is to avoid poverty and attain security. They even take hypocritical pride in their small ambition and take on a "holier than thou" attitude. Nonsense! Such people are unconsciously selfish. Is security their only purpose for living? Remember the Enlightened Triangle: Humanities/ Passion, Sexuality/ Desire, and Humor/ Health. That should be our aim in life—not fear.

ACTING FOR REAL

Fear of failure is related to desire for security. It has value only in emergencies. Many small business owners keep going for years with the aid of this motive. An emergency arises, the fear looms and they work like beavers for a spell, even doing some hard thinking until the emergency passes. Then they fall back to their former uninspired, half-hearted efforts, more concerned with petty detail than with the achievement of more substantial success. They are fortunate in that the fear cannot be maintained; they are unfortunate in that they have no better motive to inspire their efforts. Fear of any kind is ineffective in small doses, dangerous to sanity in large doses.

If fear of poverty is your sole or strongest motivator for success, the results will be equally disillusioned and convoluted. You must find a better driver.

Pride

Our pride chauffeur is closely related to our greed chauffeur (they could pass for brothers actually). The nice car with all the trimmings, paranoid driver, and on top of all that, he rarely gets anywhere because he's too busy standing in his driveway showing off his car to the neighbors. This is certainly not the chauffeur to success that you need. You'd never get out of the driveway!

Therefore, the third emotion among those not recommended as a chief motive for success is pride. This too is often the dominant motive in many moderately and temporarily successful people.

Envy, the spirit of rivalry, the desire to "keep up with the Jones's," undoubtedly inspires prodigious effort in some people and leads them to a success they might not achieve otherwise.

Pride need not be dispensed with altogether. As a complementary or subordinate motive, it has its uses. It often inspires the athlete in his training, the salesperson in outselling others, the student in making better grades, and the artist in perfecting his or her craft. In the form of professional pride, it frequently inspires the scientist to labor endlessly in the laboratory, the lawyer to win the case even for an unappreciative client, and the physician to show utmost skill in the free clinic.

But the use of pride as a chief motive is dangerous. For short bursts of effort, as in an athletic contest, a lawsuit, or stage performance, it is stimulating. But in the long run, pride, like desire for security, is a coin with a reverse side—fear of shame or humiliation.

Cultivated continuously, pride would degenerate into fear with its accompanying worries, anxieties, and conflicts of emotions. It would also turn into vanity, in which case exaggerated humiliations would keep its victim in a continual mental turmoil. Such conflict and turmoil lead quickly to inefficiency. Certainly, therefore, pride is not the emotion to cultivate as the dominant emotion to inspire your lifelong progress toward success.

Examples of the Dark Triad in Films:
A Christmas Carol, Citizen Kane, Wall Street, Ed TV, Capote

Examples of the Dark Triad in Real Life:

Howard Hughes, the stock market, The rise and fall of dot.coms, Enron

The Enlightened Triad

The second three emotions are called the Enlightened Triad. All the components of the Enlightened Triad consist of love.

"All you need is love, love…love is all you need."
—*The Beatles*

love (n.)
1. An intense feeling of tender affection and compassion.
2. Strong liking or pleasure gained from something.
3. Something that elicits deep enthusiasm in somebody.

The three emotions of the Enlightened Triad are love of work, love of people, and love of spirituality. By equally balancing them and making them our chauffeurs, these three emotions can drive us to the highest kinds of happy, content, honest, and *balanced* (be BOP) successes.

The chauffeurs in the Enlightened Triad are a diva's dream come true! They are hard-working, attentive, ambitious, and awesome drivers. They are pleasant to be around, ethical, and balanced. Their cars are elegant, immaculately tuned, comfortable, and have room for many passengers. They are always open to picking up new passengers, as needed, because they enjoy the company of strangers. These chauffeurs are passionate about their work, have great senses of humor and, believing that what goes around comes around, they treat their passengers as they themselves would like to be treated. These emotions should be your chauffeurs to success. With these guys, you can't go wrong!

We now turn from dominant emotions, which I do not recommend, and consider the motive for those which I do: love.

Love of Work

"Nothing great was ever achieved without enthusiasm."
—*Henry David Thoreau*

By this phrase, I do not mean love of drudgery or mere physical and even mental activity. I mean the love that finds its expression in creating, building, or producing. I mean the love for expressing your highest capabilities through your work. In many fields it is called the artistic impulse. Psychologists call it the desire for self-expression and maintain that none of us is altogether without it.

This is the motive that goads the great artist, the great scientists, and the genius in all fields to untiring and incessant effort. These people are so inflamed with zeal that work becomes a joy, an ecstasy. The near mania for their work energizes and inspires! They are driven to success by the joy of creation. Their very delight in their work can make them unconsciously ruthless to others as well as to themselves.

ACTING FOR REAL

As you can see, there is danger in such an impelling force. Those activated by it to a high degree are inclined to be unbalanced in other areas of life. Their families suffer from thoughtlessness, friends from selfishness, and they risk the disintegration of their support networks. As a result, they sometimes end up failing at the very thing they have put their entire hearts and souls into.

Therefore, the love of work is better as a collaborating motive rather than the dominant emotion in driving you to success. True, success can *never* be achieved without it, but it can and should be subordinated to a less dangerous source of energy. Most of us, however, are not inclined to have such an overwhelming love for our work. Consequently, we can cultivate that valuable source of energy without fear.

Love of work, when balanced by superior emotions, is one of the greatest sources of happiness and success. What joy there is in expressing ourselves fully and completely through our work! The painters and sculptors are not the only artists. We are all playing roles: the merchant is an artist in service, the sales person in selling, the comic in swaying an audience, and the detective in tracking down the criminal. The scientist, too, is an artist in discovering and applying the secrets of nature. All these people enjoy exercising their skill, expressing themselves in their work, not only for the money thus earned, but for sheer love of it as well.

In a corporation where many are cogs in a machine, the gratification of the artistic instinct is difficult. Nevertheless, those who desire it manage to find some way of expressing themselves through their work.

One, assisted or driven by feelings of pride and rivalry, perfects his speed until his production is greater than that of others. Another, often driven by strong curiosity, is constantly observing what other departments are doing—inquiring about methods of competitors and perfecting his knowledge of all aspects of the business until recognition of his superior knowledge is inevitable.

Still another of these cogs in the machine is interested not so much in information as in human beings. Books and methods do not arouse her curiosity, but human nature does. She never tires of drawing people out, listening to their opinions, and studying them. She gradually acquires an intuitive knowledge of human nature, which enables her to influence people, to win their confidence, and to inspire them to greater effort. The exercise of this skill gives her constant pleasure, for it is her means of self-expression. She is driven, just as any other artist is, to the constant improvement and use of her skill. Presently she is outstanding among her colleagues, and a leader in her company. She may be promoted to vice president of the company. Or she may be able to influence others to furnish the capital to start a new enterprise of which she herself is president.

The preceding paragraph is the story of millions of men and women who have risen from humble positions to the heads of corporations and other peaks of various ladders of status. Men and women of this type usually achieve success, for in them *two* powerful emotions are operating in harmony—love of work and love of people. They are the humanitarians. The love of their neighbors may be unconscious on their part. They may think they are interested in their neighbors for selfish reasons. But no one can drive themselves to such constant study of and interest in their neighbors unless they subconsciously love human beings. They may withhold any material gift to them, but they always give of themselves—the most valued of gifts. "The gift without the giver is bare."

An individual of this type is an artist in human nature, an expert at soothing ruffled tempers, inspiring greater effort, and winning confidence. They are builders of harmony among their fellows, producers of unity of purpose in groups, and creators of an atmosphere in which men are at ease. Subtle acts of artistry indeed.

Enough has been said, perhaps, to convince you that some phase of the instinct of self-expression has been operating in your own case, perhaps not with respect to your job, but certainly with respect to your life and who you are as a person. Perhaps your hobbies would be considered hard work or even boring to many people. It does not seem that way to you because of your emotional attitude toward it. A mere change of your emotional attitude toward your job may be all that is needed to complete success for you. Then your job will be play instead of work!

Some people may think that they must love their work because they like to spend long hours at it. But by love of your work I mean, not love of being simply busy; you are expressing the highest that is in you through your work. When there are big problems to solve, a genuine love of work will make them solvable.

Many people use work as a mere escape mechanism, an escape from frustration, from heavy thinking, and from facing their lives. They may work most of the day and be proud of it, but they are lazy nevertheless. They love only the easier work and set aside the tough problems. They have no love whatever for the mental challenge. They do not love their work enough to be open for opportunities to improve it through any kind of thought processes.

On the other hand, a far more successful person may work only a few hours a day. But in that time they tackle only the most difficult problems. And when not actually working, their mind is frequently turning back to those problems. They may get inspiration at any hour of the day or night. This person, like many successful people, is impatient with detail and routine. Yet because they have a genuine love of *hard* work, they are far more successful with their few hours of work than others are with many. It's called working smart: success intelligence! Those are the successful people—those who work with their brains more than merely their bodies.

Their work is not a mere escape mechanism, but an outlet for one's highest faculty—the creative instinct. The ultimate fulfillment of every piece of a man and woman—spiritual, mental, physical, and emotional; the creative instinct has the capability of satisfying them all.

So don't judge your love of work by the hours you put in. Long hours may only betray dislike for applying hard thinking to your work.

Now we descend upon a motive that I have been reserving: love of people. It is an even better emotion for driving you to success than love of work, and of course, a far better chauffeur than greed, fear of poverty, or pride, our Dark Triad of drivers. Whilst love of work is recommended as a driving emotion, not all of us have it naturally. Many geniuses or extremely gifted people do. But it is against ordinary human nature to love work for work's sake. Chances are you will have to love work for the sake of something else. The something else will then be your dominant emotion. What can it be? Though there are many other emotions that *occasionally* drive men to success, only three recommended drivers are so frequently effective as to deserve mention here.

Love of People

Whoever became a success by loving people? The word love has a broader meaning than most people give it. Love of people, understood in the light of its broader meaning, often *does* drive people to success.

The successful artist, business owner, or any other occupation requiring constant interaction with other people, serves people better because they put the desires of their audience and customers before themselves. Everyone knows that, in most fields, being a "good mixer" is often an important element in a person's success.

Now a person can't be a "good mixer" unless they love people, at least to a certain degree. This liking of people, the desire to mingle with them, is love and nothing else. It may be of low degree, but it needs only the addition of a desire to *serve* people to make it a love of high degree.

The most widespread form of love is *gregariousness*—the desire to mingle with others. An outgoing or gregarious person, takes initiative to socialize with others. They inspire others to do the same by letting them know that it's okay! Remember when we were children? The new kid next door would come over and say, "Do you wanna be friends?" You would say, "Okay! Mom! Can I go out and play?" It was so easy back then, but as we get older we become anxious about meeting others, self-conscious, and uncomfortable. Who makes the first phone call? Who breaks the silence to forge relationships? The gregarious person does! To mingle with our fellow men and women is a fundamental need of human nature. It is the Humanities/ Passion part of our "I AM" personality. Where this instinct is prevented, the victim sometimes becomes an extreme introvert; inferiority complexes and other psychological imbalances develop; and these are often followed by physical ills. This is the oft-loathed victim personality. Seldom does such an introvert achieve success, though they occasionally do in certain special fields of effort.

ACTING FOR REAL

But I do not accuse the introvert of not loving their fellow men and women. They often do love them, are capable of, and sometimes make heroic sacrifice for humanity. But their love is inhibited, not given free expression, and they fail to reap the rewards of such love. Instincts, including the instinct of gregariousness, demand a sufficient outlet, and punishment where the outlet is denied.

Gregariousness is the same instinct that holds sheep together in flocks, cattle in herds, and wolves in packs. Mankind is not psychologically fit for the secluded life. Nevertheless, most of us are introverts of a greater or lesser degree. Most of us will be of an intellectual state of mind, seeking to find in books a way to resolve the dissatisfaction, the emotional conflict, the sense within ourselves, to find a cure for the inefficiency and failure these bring about, through any means except the right one—the development of skills which will give adequate outlet to the gregarious instinct. Human beings rarely fare well when living in a vacuum—a state of being sealed off from external or environmental influences; isolation.

On the other hand, there will be extreme extroverts who in gregariousness seek escape from emotional conflicts arising from their work or other sources. Such people generally spend more time procrastinating from work than doing it (drinking, partying, "hanging out"). Though they love people, their love is of a low degree—it includes no great desire to serve them.

But it is rather difficult to cultivate this emotion to the proper degree unless we first learn simple gregariousness, the desire to mingle with people.

On the other hand, we will explore what can be done about the unprofitable habit of excessive introversion. Certainly this is a handicap because we cannot rise very far, cannot give our most effective service, until we can influence and affect other people.

Even in the workplace we cannot rise very far unless we develop the ability to handle other people. No matter how much ability we have, we often cannot "sell ourselves," and cannot get the opportunity to use our skills frequently and effectively—our skills in humanity, sexuality, and humor. If you can sell yourself, you can usually get the job. The sociable person ("good mixer") may fail but at least they get opportunities.

The introvert does have one advantage, however. They have good study habits and are usually better read than the extrovert. Also, they don't have the dangers of becoming too much of a social butterfly. But they must develop the social skills necessary to convince others to let them demonstrate their abilities (i.e., to get an interview, an audition).

Loving thy neighbor is not just a religious concept—it is a matter of efficiency, mental balance, and of a well-rounded and successful personality. It is a need of your nature that this love should find expression in daily social contact instead of simply existing in the wishful thinking of the introvert. To be effective in almost any walk of life, you must have the inspiration of frequent and adequate social contact, or you suffer and your work suffers.

People will distrust what you offer them unless they feel that you are one of them, familiar with their daily life and problems, even their weaknesses. A similar distrust is the cause of the general lack of success of many highly intellectual people. We sometimes have trouble relating to such people. Such people are frequently suspected of snobbery and therefore not liking "ordinary" human beings. People are always sure the "good mixer" who likes them will give them better service, and treat them better than the introvert will. The latter has a harder time at being accepted, simply because they don't give people enough opportunity to get to know and trust them. Obviously not the effective route to success!

Introverts are frequently looked upon as "wet blankets." Attempts to come out of their shells result sometimes in embarrassment and a quick retreat. They accept that the situation can't be changed and neither can they. They are simply too uninterested in other people to make a sufficient effort. What can we do to avoid this course? Well, make a little effort, of course! And do so by using humor.

Perhaps we can also wake up a little of that pride that has been there all along, but cowering in fear. Don't be defeated by this! Perhaps you can wake up a little anger. We know that we cannot depend upon mere willpower unless there is some other strong and enduring emotion behind it to drive you to do disagreeable things. Take your choice of the dominant emotions named in this book, or find some other, but find a positive driving force for yourself somewhere. Having selected one you prefer, use it to drive you to carry out the program which follows.

To begin with, let's go out and find opportunities to be a social butterfly. It may sound cheesy, but there are plenty of groups of people out there to become a part of. There's no reason to be introverted in a world filled with billions upon billions of people.

But in any social group, action, as well as presence, is necessary. Maybe you don't think you can tell a joke or be the life of the party as you feel others are. What's to prevent you from learning how? Practice telling jokes or funny stories in front of the mirror, and then in front of friends. Good storytellers are always mulling over their stories when alone—that's the secret of their success. You can do consciously what they do unconsciously. While you may consider your early attempts failures, practicing will make you more comfortable until finally it comes as naturally as anything else you enjoy doing. Rehearse, rehearse, rehearse!

Also, *think* before you speak. Ask yourself if what you are trying to say is conveying your intentions properly. Will you offend anyone? Can your comments or actions be construed as rude? Is there a better way to offer up your thoughts in a more thoughtful way?

People do not become socially acceptable without the sacrifice of a certain amount of time and effort. Learn a new hobby, sport, or skill to meet more people and make your conversations interesting. Keep up with current events, either politics, entertainment, or both! Don't be afraid to have a difference of opinion or perspective on a subject of conversation. *Listen* to what others have to say and respond with consideration for both their views and yours. People will appreciate your candor when you express yourself with openness and understanding.

Instead of looking upon simple gregariousness with contempt, as many do, believe that it is an absolute essential to the development of a greater love of yourself, others, and life. Be sure to make time for companionship, and make your responsibilities towards your relationships as important as your responsibilities for your work. How can you love anything if you don't start by loving yourself and other people? Give love, and you will reap love in return, as well as a positive feeling of pride and self-love for your own good deeds. And to truly love someone or something, love it the way it is.

They say that fear feeds upon itself, and grows abnormally. Love too, feeds upon itself and grows. Beginning with simple sociability, the growth of a higher form of love is natural and easy. But, unlike fear, love cannot grow abnormally. Love is a normal state of being, the state that puts you into harmony with all the laws of the universe, for which we are all an integral part. Love gives wings to your thoughts, inspiration to your efforts, and success to everything you do.

Having practiced being sociable until you like other people as they are, what is your next impulse? The first impulse of all love is to make others happy, to find happiness in their happiness. It is natural, therefore, that as your love increases, so does your desire to make people happy. It will not be drudgery, but a joy. You will be unhappy only if you are not helping others, or if you are working against what they are doing to better themselves. You will not be a success if you are working in reverse to hamper someone else's success. It would be like driving with one foot on the gas pedal and the other on the brake at the same time. By reaching out to help others, you are also helping yourself and you will thus be *driven* to success on a wave.

That is the secret of success that I promised you at the beginning of this book:

MYSTIC SECRET OF SUCCESS

Cultivate a love of people until your greatest desire is to make them happy. When this desire becomes an enduring passion for serving them, you will be DRIVEN to do everything necessary to succeed for yourself.

In short, only those passionately devoted to doing their best for themselves and others can expect success. Here is the dominant emotion we have been looking for, the one that is without danger to your mental well-being, the one that is in harmony with the universe and yourself, the one that can subdue conflicted emotions which otherwise lead to inefficiency, and the one that will supply the driving force necessary for long-enduring, continued application and inspired effort.

As with the other rules, let us weigh this one and see if it is confirmed by the histories of successful people. Consider, for example, a case of two amateur singers struggling to become superstars by competing for celebrity status in the star search reality television series *American Idol 2*: Clay Aiken and Ruben Studdard. Both sing popular songs and both have good voices, but one is superior in talent.

Clay sings because he enjoys it. He desires success. He is not concerned with what the audience thinks of him—many of whom make unrequited comments regarding his sexuality. He is indifferent. His primary motivation is to show off what a great singer he is.

Ruben loves his audience. His foremost thought is to make them happy, particularly the people from his hometown Birmingham, Alabama. He sings for them, connects with them, and involves them in his performances. In his desire to increase the happiness of his audience, he is always studying them. He notices immediately when they are responding and when they are not. He attentively listens to the feedback given by the judges and his audiences. First, because he enjoys it, and second, to improve upon his craft. Clay continues to get all the attention because of his superior voice, but this does not discourage Ruben. Every night, after trial and error, of love so great of singing that he cannot give it up, the audience recognizes his passion. They, too, recognize his passion and compassion for them. They love him for it. They begin to call him a big teddy bear in response to this sentiment. They begin to listen with respect, excitement, and delight every time he comes onstage. Here, they think, is a person like us—he knows us and is one of us; he knows what we like and likes it as we do. He likes us and therefore, we like him. There is inspiration in his performance that others lack. Suddenly, Ruben, the big teddy bear, becomes the season's *American Idol* champion, because the people voted and they favored more of what he had: passion and compassion.

And Ruben had no more to begin with than Clay—far less, indeed. Except he had a long-sustained, never to be denied, love of his audiences, love of his art (work) and, therefore, a dominant emotion which finally *drove* him to success.

Obviously, this story could apply to anyone in any occupation. The successful person is usually the one who is passionately devoted to his or her work and loves the public.

Love of Spirituality

Still others will be driven by their spirituality, love of God, or their devotion to a higher consciousness. While many lack this same faith and devotion, those that do have it find that it is very powerful, oftentimes more powerful than any of the other chauffeurs. That power flows from an everlasting, spiritual wellspring. What does your spirituality (of, concerned with, or affecting the soul; not necessarily pertaining to a specific religion) have to do with success? Again, love of spirituality pertains to servicing, as does love of people—servicing God, your soul, the conscious collective, humanity, nature, etc., and gives back in much the same way.

Religions, philosophies, discoveries in arts and sciences, political beliefs, and all forms of humanitarianism, are expressed through some force of emotional action, in other words, through the medium of behavior. Love of spirituality drives your expression through external behavior to get to your internal truth. A person's belief system is one that rings passionately; and as we now know, passion arouses emotion, imagination, and *drives* us. Thus, why love of spirituality is one of our recommended chauffeurs to success.

There are many examples of powerful people driven by their spirituality and humanitarianism. Mother Teresa changed the lives of millions through her belief that we are all God's creatures and therefore, should not live in poverty, or become human castoffs due to disabilities or the sorry circumstances of our birth. In an interview on poverty she said, "I see God in every human being. When I wash the leper's wounds, I feel I am nursing the Lord himself. Is it not a beautiful experience?" She recognized what she could do to serve her religious teachings, as well as the world around her, and did so by operating 517 missions in more than 100 countries, definitely dominating as a Humanities/ Passion personality! Had she not had the spiritual drive to do this, it is unlikely that she would have had the passion and devotion to change the world in the capacity in which she was able.

Mohandas Karamchand Ghandi is another notable example

of a person driven by a love of spirituality. Ghandi led the fight to end discrimination against the Indian minority in South Africa. He drew his inspiration from the teachings of the *Bhagavad-Gita*, a Sanskrit poem incorporated into the *Mahabharata*, one of the greatest religious classics of Hinduism. Other sources of his spirituality included the teachings of social theorist John Ruskin, authors and philosophers Leo Tolstoy, Ralph Waldo Emerson and naturalist Henry David Thoreau. Ghandi's own internal philosophy, expressed and symbolized by his eschewal of material possessions and nonviolent resistance, drove him to success. He returned to India with a stature equal to that of the nationalist leaders.

While many of us may be taking inventory of our own spirituality and belief systems in a quest to become the Mother Teresas and Ghandis of the future, it is necessary to understand that this great power driver does not always drive us into the world's limelight. As quoted in the 2002 *Spiderman* movie, "With great power comes great responsibility." This could not be more true. Many impassioned by their own spirituality and beliefs may do so at the expense, detriment, and abhorrence of others. Take Al Qaeda, the Islamic group, for example. Islam literally means "to surrender to the will of God." While Al Qaeda led the September 11th attacks on the U.S. in 2001, indignantly killing over 3,000 people, they did so with a passionate belief that they were serving their god and their people. Cults function in much the same way, where cult members often become their own sacrifice to satisfy the beliefs of the members' devotees. Faith and conviction in other such dogmas can have controversial imbalances and as such, are not recommended as your drivers to success. Love of spirituality can be translated into so many different varieties, including the nonreligious, that it can be confusing to know if this is one of the dominant emotions that will drive you to success. To specify, you must look at your own belief system and see how that system negatively or positively impacts other people, the environment, humanity, and the world at large. The fact that others may not share your beliefs should be respected. For our purposes, we should only choose spiritual drivers that will positively impact others, as well as ourselves, in the worldly realm. We must remember our love of people, our love of work, and keep them in balance with our love of spirituality, should we make it the leading emotion of our Enlightened Triad. Remember, you will not be a success if you are working in reverse to hamper someone else's success. Remember, don't have one foot on the gas pedal and the other on the brake!

Examples of the Enlightened Triad in Films: *Saving Private Ryan, Apollo 13, Chariots of Fire*

Examples of the Enlightened Triad in Real Life: Billy Graham, Dalai Llama, Princess Diana, Oprah Winfrey

The Six Emotions and the Creative Wheel

From the Six Dominant Emotions behind success, it's easy to transition back to the Creative Wheel of Behavior. To review, here again are the Six Dominant Emotions behind success: greed, fear of poverty, pride, love of people, love of work, and love of spirituality. The components of the McFadden Six Pack, otherwise known as the Creative Wheel of Behavior are: Power, Vulnerability, Danger, Sexuality, Humor, and Humanities. Remember how these six qualities can also easily be separated into a Dark Triad (Power, Danger, Vulnerability) and an Enlightened Triad (Humanities, Sexuality, Humor)?

Therefore:

Greed = Power/ Paranoia

Fear of Poverty = Vulnerability/ Victim

Pride = Danger/ Fear

Love of Work = Sexuality/ Desire

Love of People = Humor/ Health

Love of Spirituality = Humanities/ Passion

Plant this information in your mind, let it percolate, and commit it to memory. I guarantee that it will come in handy later—just as most pieces of information in life do.

So there you have it. You have everything you need in order to be in the right frame of mind to be the success that you have always been destined to be. The universe made it available to you for a long time—now you know where to find it and how to mine it!

Thom and his friend, Buck

CHAPTER 25
COMMUNICATION

Now that we have ourselves in tune, there is nothing more important than being able to communicate our ideas and our intentions. Communication is the means by which knowledge is imparted, needs are made known, and by which thoughts and feelings are conveyed.

com·mu·ni·ca·tion (n.)
1. the exchange of information between individuals, for example, by means of speaking, writing, or using a common system of signs or behavior.
1. a spoken or written message.
1. the conveyance of information.
1. a sense of mutual understanding and sympathy.

In these definitions, the theme of transmitting a message or the exchange of a message or information by individuals can easily be seen. Our very effective model of communication focuses on how information is processed.

VAK—Visual/ Auditory/ Kinesthetic

The human brain processes over 35,000,000 pieces of sensory information per second. We are born with and acquire filters to tune out much of this information. Each of us receives, processes, and represents this information using one predominant sense found in the acronym VAK.

ACTING FOR REAL

"VAK"
V = Visual
A = Auditory
K = Kinesthetic

Every individual has a preferred modality or representational system. We are predominantly seeing, hearing, or feeling what is going on around us. You recognize yours and other people's representational systems by listening to your and their choice of words. Visual people speak in visual terms—they see what you are showing them. Auditory people speak in auditory terms—they hear you loud and clear. Kinesthetic people speak in kinesthetic terms—they get a feel for where you are going.

Gaining the mastery of your own sensory systems is an excellent way of directing your instrument. Understanding the language of the senses (using representational systems) also makes you a persuasive communicator and a creative problem solver.

It is also important to discover what your mate's preferred representational system is (visual, auditory, or kinesthetic). The ability to "speak their language" makes communication and, ultimately, life easier. It sure helped me by realizing that my wife is visual!

We've all heard that the eyes are the windows to the soul. Within the language of the senses, eye movements indicate how other people process information. Visual people look up when they are thinking, auditory people look from side to side, and kinesthetic people look down and to the left.

VAK EXERCISES

In learning to identify the language of the senses, you will discover ways of miming it, through visual, auditory, and kinesthetic behaviors.

Listen to how your friends, family, classmates, etc. speak in general. Especially how they respond to questions. A particularly good question to ask is, "How do you know if you did a good job?" Here are some examples of response words you may hear and what they say about the person.

Who are you? Repeat the same exercise by observing yourself. Using the lists of words below, identify which is your predominant representational system. Learn to know thyself!

Visual

Words used by visual people:

Aim	Focus	Observe	Sight
Appear	View	Oversight	Get Perspective
Glimmer	Perceive	Visible	Bird's-eye view
Blind	Hazy idea	Picture	Visualize
Image	Bright idea	Portray	Watch
Imagine	Reflect	Witness	Catch a glimpse
Clarity	Inspect	Scan	Diagram
Look	See	Dim	Mind's eye

ACTING FOR REAL

A visual person might say:

Can you see my point of view?

Let me show you one of my brochures.

How does that proposal look to you?

I can foresee a long-term relationship.

Can't you just imagine yourself owning this?

Suppose you are trying to win a new business account and rewrite the following sentences so they will appeal to a visual person.

1. You're loyal to your business partners, and I respect your loyalty. Let's evaluate the differences in our services so you can understand how our company can do better for you.

2. I think you'll agree that what I've selected is the most logical one for you.

Possible answers:

1. It's **clear** to me that you are a loyal business partner, and I respect your loyalty. Let's **look** at the differences in our services so that you can **see** how our company can **focus** on better solutions for you.

2. I **imagine** you'll agree that what I have selected **appears** to be the most logical solution for you.

Auditory

Words used by auditory people:

Amplify	Eavesdrop	Proclaim	State
Announce	Express	Purr	Tell
Argue	Quiet	Tone	Give an ear to
Bark	Hush	Rap session	Tuned-in
Blabber	Idle talk	Roar	Utter
Unheard of	Converse	Say	Voice
Discuss	Inquire	Shout	Wordy
Dissonant	Listen	Silence	Noisy
Earful	Mention	Speak	

An auditory person might say:

That sounds interesting, tell me more.

Does that ring a bell?

Do you understand what I'm saying?

Rumor has it that we are the best.

Don't mention this to anyone.

Suppose you are trying to win a new business account and rewrite the following sentences so they will appeal to an auditory person.

ACTING FOR REAL

1. You're loyal to your business partners, and I respect your loyalty. Let's evaluate the differences in our services so you can understand how our company can do better for you.

2. I think you'll agree that what I've selected is the most logical solution for you.

Possible answers:

1. It **sounds** like you are a loyal business partner, and I respect your loyalty. Let's **discuss** the differences in our services so that you can **hear** how our company can **give an ear** to finding better solutions for you.

2. Let me just **say**, I think you'll agree that this solution I have selected for you is normally **unheard of.**

Kinesthetic

Words used by kinesthetic people:

Bear down on	Motion	Stir up	Get a handle on
Come to grips	Pull back	Support	Cool
Grip	Rough	Tender	Concrete
Hang tough	Rub	Tie up	Creeps
Hard	Shock	Tight	Cutting edge

Heavy	Shudder	Touch	Deep
Hot-headed	Slip up	Whip	Excite
Itch	Sore	Feel	Lukewarm
Fall apart	Hands-on	Sting	

A kinesthetic person might say:

Do you have a feel for this concept?

I need you to tackle this rough assignment.

I can pull a few strings for you.

Let's firm up this offer.

So things don't fall apart, I'd like you to take control of the situation.

Suppose you are trying to win a new business account and rewrite the following sentences so they will appeal to a kinesthetic person.

1. You're loyal to your business partners, and I respect your loyalty. Let's evaluate the differences in our services so you can understand how our company can do better for you.

2. I think you'll agree that what I've selected is the most logical solution for you.

ACTING FOR REAL

Possible answers:

1. I **feel** you are loyal to your business partners, and I respect your loyalty. Let's **pick apart** the differences in our services so that you can **get in touch** with how our company can be more **hands-on** for you.

2. You'll be very **excited** to know that I have selected the most **concrete** solution for you.

Trust and Rapport

Besides learning how to identify how others process information, an Actor for Real must also learn to build trust and rapport in order to communicate his intentions properly. While one normally would have to earn both, it is possible to instantaneously gain both trust and rapport. In addition to your attitude, being in BOP, your body language, your interest in what others have to say, and your good listening skills, it is possible to directly affect how others feel toward you through the art of pacing and modeling.

The Art of Pacing

The art of pacing is simply the matching or mirroring of any identifiable, observable behavior. Pacing is a physical technique that creates powerful levels of instantaneous rapport. It allows you to communicate clearly and effectively with others. The deep level of trust it creates makes one more receptive to your communication.

Remember at the beginning of this book, in Chapter 7, when I instructed you to watch people in restaurants? You could tell who had trust and rapport simply by watching their pacing. There are several ways you can pace a person's movements. You can do it by matching, mirroring, or crossover.

Matching —Do with your body the exact thing the other person is doing. If she crosses her right leg over her left, cross your right leg over your left. If he lifts his glass, lift yours. If they lean in, you lean in. If someone is sitting and you are standing, take a chair or squat down to communicate with them. Try this with friends or strangers and notice the response. Observe again when you are out.

Mirroring —Do with your body the same movements the other person is doing in reflection. Match someone as though they are looking in a mirror. If she is sitting across from you and crosses her right leg over her left, cross your left over your right.

Crossover —Identify a particular movement and match it with an equivalent movement of your own that conveys a similar action or motion. For example, if they cross their legs, cross your arms.

With the simple techniques of pacing, you will find that getting people "on your side" is much easier than the stress we sometimes put on it. Suppose ("magic if") that you are in a meeting trying to sell your ad campaign. You are up against some real big hitters. Your idea is good, but it is possible that someone has come up with something better. Build your enthusiasm for the presentation and use all the techniques presented in this book. Add to that the art of pacing and you are sure to make the room feel more at ease with you than they will with anyone who lacks these tools.

If you encounter resistance, you should first check yourself and how you are communicating. Eighty percent of what we convey is nonverbal. Not only can we pace with our body language, but we can also pace with our facial expressions, breathing, speech, mood, beliefs, and opinions. A smile is one of the first things you can pace with your facial expression. Breathing controls a person's internal state to a large degree. Pacing a person's breathing gives you a powerful way of building rapport with someone's internal emotional state. To do this, control your own breathing to match exactly their breathing. You can also pace someone's breathing using the crossover technique. For example, move your head slightly upwards as they breathe in, and slightly downwards as they breathe out.

Pacing speech is one of the most versatile methods of building rapport. You can use it in person or on the telephone. If a person's tone is very high or low, try to match it. If a person speaks very quickly, meet their sense of urgency by not slowing them down. Alternatively, slow your speech when communicating with a slow talker. The same is true for the volume at which a person speaks.

Are they talking softly or are they loud and boisterous? People also speak in rhythms, with ups and downs, sometimes taking long or short pauses in between words. Try to find their rhythm to get on the same frequency. You will also notice personal vocabulary, pet phrases that you can adopt in conversation. This is particularly useful when talking with youths or professionals with a trade lingo.

Mood is yet another way in which you can pace a person. Pacing someone's mood conveys understanding. Very exceptional people can even pace beliefs and opinions without compromising their own beliefs and opinions. This is far more advanced, but the notion is based on the 100 + 1% principle. Should you decide to try to pace someone's beliefs or opinions, find the 1% of the statements you can support and back it up 100-percent!

We are always communicating even if we are not speaking. Establishing trust and rapport is the most essential element in life. Pace to build trust and rapport and then lead. Pace to subconsciously grab the attention of a room and then hold it. Pacing works because it puts you in agreement, on the same page, as the person or people you are dealing with. This level of agreement creates a conditioned response of saying, "Yes!—yes, I like you, yes, I will work with you, yes, I will date you, and yes, you can!"

ACTING FOR REAL

Modeling

Modeling is another important tool to earn trust and rapport. If you model success, then you'll become a successful role model. The attitude and game plan employed by the masses to create positive change relies on trial and error. This approach wastes time, energy and money in a losing effort. Most of us have neither unlimited time nor money. Our decision to proceed on a journey toward change without a specific blueprint for success accounts for a high casualty rate. By contrast, we recognize time as a limited and irreplaceable asset and create a strategy of *modeling* to dramatically reduce time, save money, and increase our chances for success.

Modeling, as the name implies, involves selecting a person, situation or experience that is time-tested for success and then duplicating every possible detail to ensure that all the characteristics of the successful model are captured and applied to you.

There are many examples of modelers. Rich Little, the famous comedian and impersonator, modeled the voices of Ronald Reagan, James Stewart and John Wayne so convincingly that he sounded more like them than they did. Modeling enables you to have the benefit of success while remaining unique, by *observing* and *enhancing*. Japanese companies modeled American products and then enhanced them. The Japanese method was based on careful observation, key questions, careful attention to answers and repetition of that process, followed by quick and decisive action. The Japanese approach followed the four steps of modeling:

1. Observation
2. Probing questions
3. Careful listening
4. Taking decisive action

Remember, knowledge without action is simply information. Study others who have had success in whatever it is you desire to do, then do it!

Other Keys to Build Trust & Rapport

Become Genuinely Interested in Other People—Regardless of the physical assets you or your company may have, it's the people who will make you successful. They are your key asset and getting to know them should be as natural as knowing the technical aspects of your job. Being genuine is the key here. Don't play games by getting to know others only for your own personal gain. Getting to know each other should be mutually beneficial.

Smile—Whether you're pleasant to be around or not depends not on the situation, but on you. Image is created by such seemingly minor considerations.

ACTING FOR REAL

Remember a Person's Name—is to them, the sweetest and most important sound in the world.

Be a Good Listener—Encourage others to talk about themselves. Informed people run on information and what better way to find out what's going on than to follow this principle. Listen with everything you've got. How you listen says volumes about whether your interests are about you or something other than yourself.

Talk in Terms of the Other Person's Interest—We are all thinking about ourselves most of the time. Why not create a stronger professional image by putting away our own concerns for a while and talking about what others are thinking?

Make the Other Person Feel Important—Do it sincerely— "Make dealing with you important to me, and I will work hard for you." Much of our professional image rests with our coworkers. When our dealings let them see that we appreciate their contributions to what is achieved, we are building a strong bond that will withstand the pressures of day-to-day struggles.

Every Actor for Real Should Have Three Nonprejudiced, Clean Jokes—This is vital, whether or not humor is a part of your triangle. The ability to tell a joke well is the ability to connect intimately with your audience whether they are in a darkened theater, across from your desk at the office, or appearing on a monitor. Telling a joke involves specific timing, voice inflection, certain stylization of words, and the ability to read whether or not the audience is following in every moment. If any of those components drop, for even a moment, the audience is lost and the joke falls flat instantly. The successful Actor for Real will spend at least a couple of hours every week practicing telling jokes, whether to friends, family, coworkers, or even better, strangers.

You now have all the tools you need to be a rising star in your life. You have learned the keys to building empowering characters in your day-to-day activities and for the long term. You have built character. You are a work in progress, but you will be an ever-rising star by continually working on yourself and employing these new skills. Not only will you shine in your own life, but you will shine in others as well, inspiring equal effort on the parts of others. Your new attitude, your presence, your awareness, your thoughtfulness, your reliability from being driven, and your powers of communication, will all tell a story for which you can be proud!

ACTING FOR REAL

WORDS ARE AN ACTOR FOR REAL'S GREATEST TOOLS
—EXERCISE

It is required of all my students to memorize the following text. As an Actor for Real, you too, should commit it to memory. I have saved this exercise for last because if you learn this text and apply to it everything you have learned in this book, it will literally change your life!

<u>Words Are an Actor for Real's Greatest Tools</u>

For me words have color, character; they have pouts, faces, manners, gesticulations. They have moods, humor, eccentricities; they have tints, tones, personalities…

Because people cannot see the color of words, the tint of words, the secret ghostly motions of words…

Because they cannot hear the whispering of words, the rustling of the procession of letters, the dream-flutes and dream-drums, which are thinly and weirdly played by words…

Because they cannot perceive the pouting of words, the raging of and racketing of words…

Because they are insensible to the phosphorescing of words, the fragrance of words, the tenderness or hardness; the dryness or juiciness of words…the interchange of values in gold, silver and the copper of words…

Is that any reason why we should not try to make them hear or to make them see or to make them feel?

Once you have read through this text, you need to score it, pick it apart, make it your own. What characters can you portray with the use of this text? What qualities can you apply?

Some examples:

"For me, **(Humanities/ Passion)** words have color…

"… they have pouts **(Sexuality),** faces **(Humor)**…"

"…the raging and racketing of words…" **(Danger/ Fear/ auditory)**

"…the phosphorescing **(visual)** of words…"

"…the fragrance **(olfactory)** of words…"

"…the tenderness or hardness **(kinesthetic)** of words…"

Recite "Words…" while conveying these different personalities and qualities. Add gestures to your speech. Use behavior, modeling, vary your tone, your volume, your pace. Try reciting it in many different ways. Use your Power/ Danger personality the whole way through, then try the same using your Humor/ Health personality. Try all the personalities in the Creative Wheel of Behavior. Then intermingle them. Notice how the different behavior changes the meanings of the words. Become aware of how your gestures impact a sentence. Discern how your pace and volume add or take away power from the context. Use what you learn with this text in your own life, in your own words. Become mindful of how your every move and every breath shapes your words. Words are an Actor for Real's greatest tools. Remember,

ACTING FOR REAL

80-percent of what we convey is nonverbal, so it is not the words themselves that are the most important, but rather, it is the way that we use them. Learn this, through repetition of this exercise, and you will be empowered.

It is up to you, the Actor for Real, to make people see, to make them feel, or to move them in order to engage them more fully in your life.

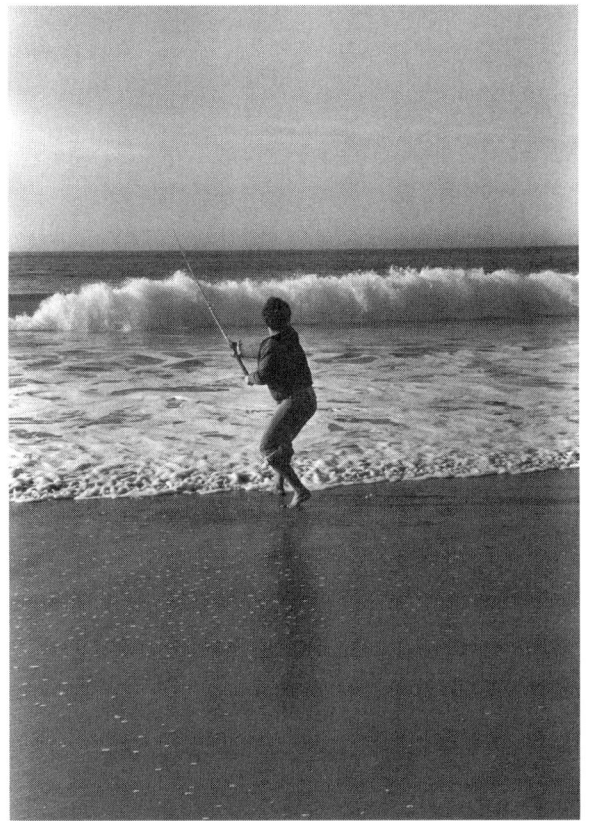

Be Persistent! Never give up!
Photo by Brian Hamill

*"Give a man a fish; you have fed him for today. Teach
a man to fish; and you have fed him for a
lifetime"—Chinese Proverb*

CHAPTER 26
SELF-PERSEVERANCE

*"Nothing in the world can take the place of persistence. Talent will
not; nothing is more common than unsuccessful men with talent.
Genius will not; unrewarded genius is almost a proverb. Education
will not; the world is full of educated derelicts. Persistence and
determination are omnipotent."*

—Calvin Coolidge

ACTING FOR REAL

The mystic formula for success is now before you. To be a success, simply live according to the principles outlined in preceding chapters. Write your life's screenplay based upon them, and then act it out. Stick to it! The show must go on! Script your program and read it every day in rehearsal for life and inspiration for your performance. Read the quotes throughout the chapters to inspire you. Perseverance is the hardest part, as with every challenging endeavor; but I have pointed out certain things which will make it easier, the chief of which is the cultivation of your abiding passion for yourself, your work, and your fellow people.

The following course of action is a suggestion to stimulate your thinking. Modify each step to suit yourself and your particular talents and needs. The finished product, your blockbuster life, will then be your own blueprint upon which you can build with enthusiasm.

STEP 1: If you are not now serving the public or a part of it in some way, start doing it at once.

Nearly everyone earning money, whether at a job, in business, a profession, or in almost any other way, is already serving—a fact which shows the fundamental necessity for this step. So Step I is particularly beneficial for the soon to be employed, students exploring potential careers, or people looking to make a career change. It is also beneficial for those looking to be more gregarious, to meet new people, and interested in learning about new things. Step I immediately contributes to nurturing your Humanities/ Passion personality, the most powerful character in the McFadden Six Pack. The following are suggestions to begin serving the public:

a) Choose to volunteer for a charity in a field of service that interests you and where you are most likely to serve best.

b) Prepare yourself for efficient service in that field.

c) Learn to know people, through habits of gregariousness, so that you will better know how to make people happy.

d) Practice the art of making people happy whenever opportunity offers.

e) Pursue and serve continuously in community activities and charity work.

f) Join organizations outside of your normal groups to meet different people.

g) Get to know people who you may collaborate with later in life. Look ahead of their path to see where you may meet again.

As we have learned, people will not accept the service you may later offer unless they feel that you know them, understand them, and are one of them.

STEP II. If you have a job or trade that you are now working in, always be striving to improve or change it and reach more people

ACTING FOR REAL

by continuously studying and practicing your craft. You must be BOP—Balanced, Observant and Present at all times.

This step is necessarily vague because there are so many kinds of jobs and services out there, but being BOP is universal and can be applied to anyone in and out of the workforce. Write out your own Step II in detail so you will know where to aim your focus and attention.

Initially, you may just desire to serve people (humanitarian) rather than your work, but must wait to gain the necessary trust to do this. In the meantime, you can gain skill and a better knowledge of people by volunteering your time as a way of publicity and continued improvement in yourself. This action will cultivate your Humanities/ Passion personality, as well as put you in a better position in your career.

STEP III. Cultivate a strong, enduring, acceptable, dominant emotion, which will drive you, regardless of the work involved, the sacrifices you have to make, and disappointments and discouragements along the way. Choose a driving emotion that will constantly be moving you forward, year after year, on the path you have chosen, until you have reached your purpose. If you do not know where to start, look to the recommended drivers of the Enlightened Triad that begin with love. And always check your attitude. A chauffeur will not drive a passenger with a bad attitude!

Without a driving power, Steps I and II, and *all other* steps, will be like New Year's resolutions, entered upon with enthusiasm, but soon forgotten and neglected. You will become a casualty! Only such a driving power can give you utmost efficiency and prevent constant indecision, which causes inefficiency. Only a driving force within you can inspire you to make your own program and follow it, to think day and night until the necessary ideas, means, and plans come to you and inspire you to make the required effort and application—which no mere book or anything else in all the world, can provide you. With such a driving emotion, you will *find your own way to success*, you will never rest until you do; and you will need neither my help nor anyone else's. With such a driving emotion, you will discover for yourself what to do, and you will do it. With such a driving emotion, barring illness and other unforeseen circumstances, you will be successful in spite of yourself.

The three driving emotions from the Dark Triad may be considered for temporary gain, but be careful not to choose one of them until you have seriously considered my warnings about them. Again, these are:

1. Greed
2. Fear of Poverty
3. Pride

ACTING FOR REAL

Though envy, revenge, and many other emotions occasionally serve as the driving power for more or less limited success, the only generators of success worth considering in most cases are the three from the Enlightened Triad that we discussed:

4. Love of Work
5. Love of People
6. Love of Spirituality

I do recommend love of work, but it too has its dangers. Love of people and love of spirituality are recommended with qualification: that they are accompanied by no dangers, whatsoever. Choose any *one* of the last three as your generator of success, cultivate it, and your life story will be a page-turner!

Most people, because of their reluctance to accept the practicality of idealism, will probably first try to cultivate a love of work. When they experience difficulty in maintaining the emotion, they will try love of people. It is easier to love your work if you love the people that it serves.

It may be argued that many idealists are not successful. This is simply because they do not apply the driving power of their ideals to their daily work. They look upon the latter as something separate. They have somehow been given the idea that making money, even through service, is objectionable, or that their job or business is without merit because they get paid for their work. The conflict of emotions aroused by such false ideas causes inefficiency, made worse by the very strength of their ideals. There is no reason why you should not make money doing something you love!

STEP IV. Find a means for renewing your enthusiasm whenever it lags. Stop your negative self-talk, your inner critic and edit your life. Use your success intelligence. Don't become casual. Commit to commit!

Some people will find means of inspiration to continue acting in books or seminars, others in religion or spirituality. Some will find it in music, others in contact with people. Still others will be inspired through the examples of others. You must find your means by yourself. If you do not find it at first, look again—somewhere else! Remember, you are a work in progress, and you must work to progress!

STEP V. If your enthusiasm should still lag, ponder seriously whether you are in the right profession, surrounding yourself with the right people, and honoring your own thoughts, beliefs and values. You must be true to your essence, your source point. Our external behaviors must be connected with our internal truth in order to bring success.

If necessary, changes you have to make are worth every sacrifice; but try all the other steps before giving up skills and support you have already acquired. Here, you must be careful, "The grass is *always* greener on the other side." But if you definitely and permanently dislike your work, your associates, or have an ethical distaste for what you are doing, then almost any change is a change for the better. *For great success, you must have passion!*

STEP VI. On your way to a position of power, either in your personal life, business or other, associate with people of quality, people who can teach you something. Outside ideas and training should always complement and benefit your own. Surround yourself with role models and people with good attitudes, people who are in BOP, attaining to be their best and not afraid to nurture their Humanities, Sexuality and Humor personalities. Spend quality time with quality people! If you spend quality time with "casual" people, you end up as a casualty!

Enlisting or hiring another person's experience is the shortest road to success. This also applies to socializing, working and practicing your skills alongside others who can help you while you help them. But be sure your alliances have the experience you need, and have been successful in the work, or in their lives, in which you engage with them. Some of the greatest successes I know of do not have too much ability. Some have had little education, but they do know how to choose and delegate to people with experience and skills to do much of their work for them.

The same principles hold true, no matter with whom you choose to have a livelihood. Join forces with people who can teach you, and *allow yourself to be taught—be coachable!* Don't think that you know all there is to know about life, your profession, your hobbies, politics, etc. You may also need people who may not know as much as you, but know something different. Don't let your ego, your Power personality, put restrictions upon the service you give to the public. You can never know so much, even about your own business, that there is no more to learn.

Your contemporaries can help you in business by keeping on top of the industry that you work in, by bringing in their experience gained before meeting you, and by their acquired outside ideas and training that can be added to yours. They know not only what you have taught them, but something different which can increase the efficiency of your service, the contentment of your audience, or the breadth of your market. Such people may be rare but they are out there. Figuratively audition them, and cast them for a part in your life!

Also, as an Actor for Real, be your own director. Make sure that you are living up to your part. Let your life's cast contribute their ideas about your performance. Do you give your contemporaries a chance to educate you? If someone is an "outsider" in your world, will you let him or her lead you? Will you let them have a guest starring role in your life? If not, your peers will soon be forging ahead of you on the road to success—while leaving you behind. Why should they let you guest star in their life, when you keep

hogging all the roles in yours? Let others have their limelight too, along with your encouragement. Don't be afraid to let them give you guidance. Be coachable! Many a simple, unpretentious person has risen to the highest levels of success through collaboration and guidance by others. And that brings us back full circle to where we set off at the beginning of this book.

STEP VII: Return to the beginning of this book, and keep on returning to it throughout your run in life! Rediscover the Creative Wheel of Behavior and your Creative Triangle. Continue to tune your instrument and be BOP until you hear the fat lady sing!

Whatever you do, do it 100% or don't do it at all.

If you haven't developed your personal success plan yet, now is the time to start doing it. Write your life's screenplay, cast yourself as the star, and start acting it out—and you will be a successful Actor for Real! Now, go break a leg!

APPLAUSE!...

Thom's Top Ten for Being an Actor for Real

1.   You will receive a body. You may not like it, but it's the only one you're going to get.

2.   You are enrolled in a full-time informal school called Life. Each day in this school you will have the opportunity to learn lessons. You may like the lessons or you may think them irrelevant and stupid. You will learn that life is simple, but not easy.

3.   In this world there are no mistakes, only life's lessons, which are the outcomes that you cause by your decisions. Personal growth is a process of trial, error, and experimentation. The failed experiments of life are as much a part of the growth process as the experiment that ultimately works.

4.   Over "there," is no better than over "here." When your over "there" has become an over "here," you will simply obtain another "there" that will again look better than "here." Who's on first where the grass is greener again?

5.   Others are mirrors of yourself. Often something you see in others reflects something you love or hate about yourself. You cannot love others unless you first learn to love yourself. Hating others is a sign you have not learned the lesson of being good to yourself first. You can never be free of hate until you learn to love those you hate. This does not mean you have to associate with them.

6.   What you make of your life is up to you. You have all the tools and resources you need. The choice is yours. Carve out your career.

7.   So the key to the possibility of obtaining our true power lies in our ability to change our beliefs. It's like, "Which comes first, the chicken or the egg?" "You do." We are limited only by our own imagination.

8.   Although we can do anything we desire our motivation is determined by our state of awareness.

9.   Find the reward of someone's behavior, then you will better understand what motivates them.

10. Although we don't always like what others do, we should only judge them by their own standards, not ours. Stop being a critic. It all comes back to you eventually.